Lotus

Illustrated DICTIONARY of PHILOSOPHY

Complied and Edited by:
Sable Brown

AF520328

Lotus PRESS
4735/22, Prakash Deep Building
Ansari Road, Daryaganj,
New Delhi - 110002

Lotus Illustrated

DICTIONARY of PHILOSOPHY

All right reserved. No part of this publication may be copied, reproduced, stored in a retrieval system or transmitted in any form or by any means without specific prior permission of the publisher.

© Lotus Press: 2016

ISBN 81 89093 52 5

Published by:

Lotus Press Publishers & Distributors
Unit No. 220, 2nd Floor, 4735/22,
Prakash Deep Building, Ansari Road, Darya Ganj,
New Delhi- 110002, Ph.: 32903912, 23280047, 09811838000
• E-mail : lotuspress1984@gmail.com www.lotuspress.co.in

Printed at : Lotus Press Publishers & Distributors, New Delhi

Preface

Philosophy is generally perceived as difficult. One of the reasons for this general perception is no doubt the abstruse language that the philosophers use. But philosophers do not make their knowledge difficult so that it would be less accessible to the multitude. Their task forces them to employ and create terminology far from everyday language.

The three main divisions in philosophy are Metaphysics, Epistemology and Logic. Metaphysics is the study of all that is in the world. Under this heading are studied the classification of existing beings. In Epistemology, we study the foundations of knowledge and various sciences, like how we acquire knowledge and when, if ever, we can be sure that we know something. Logic, the third part, deals with the deductive method of proofs. It is the most certain part of philosophy and has reached a high level of sophistication with the invention of prepositional calculus or symbolic logic.

There are many schools of philosophy which deal with the above-mentioned questions. Some of them have existed for a very long time. Some are theistic and believe in divinity and divine revelation. Some are atheists and materialist, meaning that they believe in gaining knowledge through their senses. Some stress the positive role that senses play in acquiring information, while others believe that the brain reflects the world as it is. Some schools prefer to study society and hope to change history, while others look for the salvation of the individual.

And with every school, there are associated typical words, which may have meanings different from their everyday use. It is necessary to give both context and meaning and that is what this dictionary attempts to cover.

abduction
a heuristic procedure that reasons inductively from available empirical evidence to the discovery of the probable hypothesis that would best explain its occurrence.

absolute
a term used to cover the totality of what really exist. A totality of thought as a unitary system somehow generating all apparent diversity.

absolute space
space considered as an entity within which bodies are placed, and which itself has real properties, such as shape or extension.

absolutism
a philosophical doctrine that is opposed to any form of relativism. In ethics this doctrine insists that values are objectively real.

absorption (Abs.)
a form of argument expressed as p. q, thus, p (p.q.). For example: If Mary comes to the party, so will George. Therefore, if Mary comes to the party then both George and Mary will.

abstraction
the process of forming a general concept by omitting every distinguishing feature from our notions of some collection of particular things. For example, the idea of 'green' could in principle, be derived by abstracting from one's specific experiences of a summer lawn, the leaves of trees, and emeralds. In recent works efforts are made to understand the status of abstract ideas focussing on the analysis of general terms in language.

absurd
1. contrary to reason or beyond the limits of rational thought.

2. paradoxical, nonsensical or meaningless.

abunaser
latinised form of the name of Persian philosopher al-Farabi.

accent, fallacy of
an informal fallacy that arises from the ambiguity produced by a shift of emphasis in spoken or written language.

acceptance
one possible reaction to a theory or to evidence.

accident

1. a feature that something happens to have but that it might not have had.
2. the informal fallacy of applying a generally reliable rule to a particular case without considering the qualifying features that might make it an exception to the rule.
3. unlimited applicability to every instance would follow syllogistically only if the rule were a genuinely universal proposition, the truth of which is often difficult to defend in practical cases. Merely probable guidelines are easier to establish as 'rules of thumb,' but they do not deserve to be applied indiscriminately.

acosmism

a doctrine that the world is unreal and only God exists.

acrasia or akrasia

a Greek term for 'weakness of the will'. Aristotle distinguished a man who is morally weak (akrates) from a man who can resist the temptations of sensuous pleasures (enckrates).

act / rule utilitarianism

distinction between ways of applying the greatest happiness principle for the moral evaluation of actions on utilitarian grounds. Act-utilitarianism supposes that each particular action should be evaluated solely by reference to the merit of its own consequences, while rule-utilitarianism considers the consequent value of widespread performance of similar actions.

action theory

branch of philosophy concerned with the analysis of what human beings do intentionally. This typically includes an effort to distinguish actions from mere events and some proposal concerning the ethical significance of actions. Understanding the relation between choice or volition and the performance of an action.

action at a distance

a remote and instaneous influence by the body, without any apparent mechanism for transmitting the force produced.

■ activism

according to activism, reality (natural as well as social) can be explained in terms of action or praxis. In opposition to intellectualism, activism emphasises that action precedes the intellect.

■ actuality and potentiality

actuality (Greek: energeia) refers to that mode of being in which a thing can bring other things about or be brought about by them, the realm of events and facts. By contrast, potentiality (Greek: dynamis) refers to not a mode in which a thing exists, but rather the power to effect change, the capacity of a thing to make transitions into different states.

■ adaptation

a process of quick adjustment to the conditions of external or internal environment. This concept was made use of by scientists as well as sociologists.

■ Addams, Jane

American pragmatist and social worker. Distressed by the dismal living conditions endured by women, minorities, and the working poor, Addams established Hull House in Chicago as a social settlement in 1889 and campaigned tirelessly for women's suffrage, world peace, and economic justice. Her address to the Chicago Liberty Meeting, Democracy or Militarism (1899) and the pamphlet Why Women Should Vote (1909) are representative expressions of her belief that women should properly exert a pacifistic influence on American political life. Addams's writings on social issues include Democracy and Social Ethics (1902) Newer Ideals of Peace (1907), A New Conscience and an Ancient Evil (1911), Twenty Years at Hull House (1912), The Larger Aspects of the Women's Movement (1914), and Women, War, and Suffrage (1915). Addams shared the 1931 Nobel Prize for peace.

■ addition (Add.)

a basic argument form expressed as p, thus p V q. For example, 'It is raining. Therefore, either it is raining or the sun is shining.' Although its use in ordinary thought is notably rare, this pattern of reasoning serves a vital role in the construction of formal proofs in many systems of logic.

ad hoc

Latin phrase, meaning 'to this' suggests the directional character of the ad hoc. In the logic of explanation an ad hoc hypothesis is one formed to explain a given phenomenon, but different from powerful hypothesis in not being derivable from other phenomena or yielding other testable consequences.

ad hominem argument (argument against the person)

the informal fallacy of supposing that a proposition should be denied because of some disqualifying feature of the person who affirms it. This fallacy is the mirror image of the appeal to authority. In its abusive form, ad hominem is a direct (and often inflammatory) attack on the appearance, character, or personality of the individual.

a dicto simpliciter ad dictum secundum quid

a non-verbal fallacy that occurs when a general rule is applied to a special case without taking special circumstances into consideration.

adiafora [adiaphora]

Greek term used by the classical Stoics to designate actions that are morally indifferent.

One does not have any direct obligation either to perform or to avoid such actions, even when they might indirectly affect our general well-being.

Adler, Alfred (1870-1937)

influenced by the philosophy of Hans Vaihinger, Adler's 'individual psychology' focussed on the efforts people invariably make in order to compensate for their (self-perceived) inferiority to others, whether it originally arose from a specific physical defect, relative position in the family constellation, particular experiences of humiliation, or a general lack of social feeling for others.

■ **adoptionism**

the theological doctrine that Christ, born as a mortal being, became the son of God by adoption.

■ **Adorno, Theodor Wiesengrund (1903-1969)**

German musicologist, social critic and political philosopher, author of Philosophie der neuen Musik (The Philosophy of Modern Music) (1949) and Noten zur Literatur (Notes to Literature) (1958-74). A leading member of the Frankfurt school, Adorno traced the development and failure of Western reliance on reason in Dialektik der Aufklärung (Dialectic of Enlightenment) (1947). In The Authoritarian Personality (1951) Adorno described the ways conformity to the demands of social propriety imposes paradox and contradiction on the lives of individual human beings. Negative Dialektik (Negative Dialectics) (1966) openly defends the critical task of exposing, dissolving, and undermining the harmful influence of rigid conceptual schemes.

■ **adventitious ideas**

refers to one of Descartes, three classes of ideas, along with 'factitious' and 'innate'. Adventitious ideas come from experience, entering the mind through sensation.

■ **Aeolus**

ruler of the winds, dwelling, according to Homer, on a floating island.

■ **aeon**

among Valentinia Gnostics, especially, the name given to the semi-divine, spiritual intermediaries emanating from God and the material world, which meant—in their view—bridging between good and evil.

■ affect

a term used in the rational psychology of Spinoza to name the variety of feelings, purposes, and drives which motivate us. As the affects are internal their influence upon us would seem to allow a kind of self-determination.

■ affectivity

properties possessed by things affect the sense organs to generate percepts. Kant used the term 'affectivity' to denote the power of properties of things to act on the sense organs.

■ affirmative conclusion from negative premise

the formal fallacy committed in a categorical syllogism that violates a syllogistic rule by having an affirmative conclusion derived from at least one negative proposition as a premise.

■ affirmative proposition

a statement whose prepositional quality is determined by its assertion that some or all members of one class of things are also included as members of some other class.

■ affirming the alternative

A fallacious inference in the form of p q pq. For example, 'The softball team will win either Tuesday's game or Thursday's. It will win Tuesday's game. Therefore, it will not win Thursday's game.'

■ affirming the consequent

a fallacy having the form p q, q p. For example, 'If Dole had been elected President in 1996, then he would no longer be a Senator. Dole is no longer a Senator. Therefore, Dole was elected President in 1996.'

■ a fortiori

'to the stronger', or 'even more so'. We are abound to accept an a fortiori claim because of our prior acceptance of a weaker application of the same reasoning or truth.

■ after image

refers to the visual version of what psychologists call 'after-sensation', wherein a visual image resembling an observed object persists after the external stimulus assumed to have caused it has been withdrawn.

■ **agape**

Greek term which means 'selfless love'. The term is derived from the Agape or 'love feast' of the early Christians, a common meal to promote 'Christian fellowship' frequently associated with the sacrament.

■ **agni**

a Sanskrit term which means 'fire'. One of the most important of the Vedic gods, Agni was god of the altar fire and also represented the trinity of the earthly fire, lightening and Sun.

■ **agent**

a person who performs an action. Ethical conduct is usually taken to presuppose the possibility that individual human agents are capable of acting responsibly.

■ **agnosticism**

belief that human beings do not have sufficient evidence to warrant either the affirmation or the denial of a proposition. The term is used especially in reference to our lack of knowledge of the existence of god.

■ **agreement, method of**

one of Mill's methods for discovery of causal relationships. If a specific antecedent circumstance is found to be present on every occasion on which a phenomenon occurs, it may be inferred to be the cause of that phenomenon.

■ **aisqhsiV [aisthêsis]**

Greek term for sense perception, the epistemic significance of which was vigorously debated. The Eleatics argued that mere sensation is inferior to nohsiV [nóêsis], while Empedocles and the Atomists regarded it as a vital connection with the natural world. Plato took perception to be unreliable as a source of knowledge, since it deals only with temporal objects. For

Aristotle, on the other hand, aisqhsiV is a basic activity of living organisms, through which they acquire information about material things.

aition [aition]

the most general Greek term for cause or responsibility, used by Aristotle especially in reference to any one of the four kinds of answer it is legitimate to give in response to any 'Why . . . ?' question.

akrasia [akrásia]

literally, 'bad mixture,' the Greek term for the character flaw of incontinence or weakness of the will, the condition in which an agent is unable to perform actions that are known to be right. Although Socrates apparently held that doing good follows directly from knowing what is good, Aristotle believed akratic human behaviour to be commonplace, and offered an extended account of its origin and consequences.

Albert the Great (1206-1280)

German Dominican philosopher and Bishop of Ratisbon. Revered by his contemporaries as 'doctor universalis' for the breadth of his philosophical knowledge, Albert tried to synthesise many disparate philosophical positions from the tradition but also encouraged empirical study as a source of knowledge of the natural world. He is remembered chiefly as the teacher and colleague who encouraged Thomas Aquinas to apply Aristotelian arguments to Christian thought.

alchemy

a mediaeval philosophy which combines an occult cosmology with practical chemical experimentation.

Alexander, Samuel (1859-1938)

Australian-English philosopher. Alexander defended perceptual realism as an alternative to the idealism of his contemporaries. His theory regarding the 'emergent evolution' of mind within the natural order, proposed in Space, Time, and Deity (1920), was similar in many respects to the views of Henri Bergson. Alexander also developed a thorough axiology in Beauty and other Forms of Value (1933). During his tenure at Manchester, Alexander helped Zionist colleague Chaim Weizmann secure the Balfour agreement, an initial step towards creation of the modern state of Israel.

■ Alexandrian school

the term used for a centre of Neo-platonism in 5th and 6th century Alexandria. Unlike its rival at Athens the Alexandrian School became Christian, concentrating on scholarly commentary rather than the urgy and metaphysical speculation. It survived the capture of Alexandria by the Arabs (641AD) and transmitted much Neo-platonist learning to the Middle Ages.

■ alfenaus

a mediaeval term which distinguishes certain adjectives that have peculiarly tight relations with the nouns to which they are applied.

■ algebra of logic

name applied in the 19th century to the development, influenced by mathematics, beyond traditional logic.

■ algorithm

derived from Al-Khwarizmi of Al-Korisimi, the surname of the author of a famous 9th-century Arabic work on arithmetic which was translated into Latin. All such books were called the Algorismus, and so the term came to mean the operations of arithmetic in Arabic notation. It now refers to any sort of logical or mathematical operation with any sort of notation.

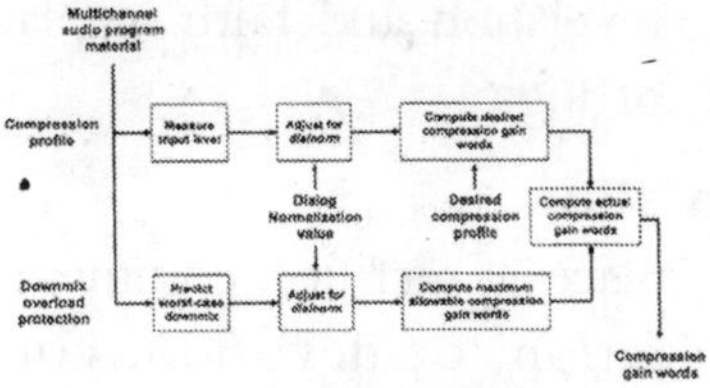

■ alhqeia [alêtheia]

Greek word for truth, which generally marks the distinction between doxa [dóxa] (mere belief) and episthmh [epistêmê] (genuine knowledge) in the philosophy of Plato. According to Aristotle, truth appears in our propositional judgements, whose logical structure mirrors the nature of things.

■ alienation (Ger. Entäusserung or Entfremdung)
extreme separation from one's own nature, from the products of one's labour, or from social reality, which often results in an indifference or outright aversion toward some aspect of life that might otherwise be attractive and significant.

■ alogism
denial of logical thinking as a means to arrive at the truth. Alogism substitutes intuition, revelation and faith in place of logic.

■ altar
place of sacrifice, commemoration, or devotion, commonly shaped like a table.

■ alternation
logical relation holding between propositions at least one of which is true.

■ alternative occurrence
complex event comprising the occurrence of one or the other (or both) of its constituent events.

■ Althusser, Louis (1918-1990)
Algerian-French social philosopher. In Pour Marx (For Marx) (1965), Lénin et la philosophie (Lenin and Philosophy) (1969) and Lire le Capital (Reading Capital) (1970), Althusser offered a structuralist re-interpretation of the later works of Marx. According to Althusser, social organisation is determined wholly by ideological consequences expressed in economic and political power, enforced in home and family as well as in the workplace. The differential roles to which individuals are assigned in a society, he argued, are clearly signified not only by the presence of particular notions in its cultural paradigms, but even more dramatically by the absence of others. Elements d'autocritique (Essays in Self-Criticism) (1974) includes retractions from many of these central themes.

■ altruism
belief that an agent's moral decisions should be guided by consideration for the interests

and well-being of other people rather than merely by self-interest, as egoism would recommend.

■ amazons

the 'breastless ones', a mythical race of female warriors dwelling in Asia Minor. Their right breasts were said to have been cut off to facilitate use of the bow. They were ruled by a queen, and mated periodically with men of another race. Male children were exposed at birth.

■ ambiguity

the presence of two or more distinct meanings for a single word or expression. In itself, ambiguity is a common, harmless, and often amusing feature of ordinary language. When unnoticed in the context of otherwise careful reasoning, however, it can lead to one of several informal fallacies.

■ ampliative

from Latin ampliare which means 'to make wider'. 'Ampliative judgement' are 'synthetic judgement' have identical in meaning, referring to judgements whose predicates have been not implict in the meanings of their subject terms.

'Ampliative inference' on the other hand refers to the type of inference in which something predicated in the conclusion is not found in the premises.

■ amoral

having no bearing on, declining to be influenced by, or making no reference to, moral values or judgements.

■ amphiboly

informal fallacy that can result when a sentence is ambiguous because of its grammatical structure, even if all of its terms are clear.

■ anacreontic

verse in praise of wine and women in the manner of the Greek poet Anacreon.

■ anagogical interpretation

refers to interpretations, usually of scripture, leading one 'upward'. The anagogical has been thus a type of allegorical interpretation.

■ analogia entis

a Latin term which means 'analogy of being'.

■ analogy

similarity in several respects between discrete cases. A logical argument by analogy relies upon an inductive inference from the supposition that things are similar in certain known respects to the likelihood that they are also similar in some further unknown respect.

■ analysis

process of breaking up a complex concept or expression in order to reveal its simpler constituents, thereby elucidating its implicit meaning. The significance and value of this method is challenged by the paradox that analyses are bound either to be inadequate trivial and uninformative.

■ analysis, intentional

a type of analysis introduced by Husserl taking the intentional aspect of experience to be fundamental, and exhibiting the development of all philosophy from this starting point.

■ analysis, philosophical

analytic function of philosophy consists of translating sentences into other sentences which contain neither the key words of the original sentences, nor synonyms for them.

■ analytic

from the Greek analytikos, derived from the verb analyein, 'to resolve into its elements'.

■ analytic judgement, statement, or proposition

a judgement, statement, or proposition with the properties of necessity and universality by virtues of the fact that the predicate of the judgement is a result of analysis of the subject term.

■ analytic/synthetic
distinction between judgements or propositions. A judgement is analytic if the concept of its predicate is already contained in that of its subject. if the concepts of its subject and predicate are independent, it is synthetic.

■ analytic philosophy
twentieth-century methods of philosophising, generally characterised by careful effort to uncover logical and philosophical suppositions concealed beneath the superficial structure of statements in ordinary uses of language, pursuit of clarity in the treatment of genuine philosophical issues, and a deep respect for the achievements of natural science.

■ anamnhsiV [anámnêsis]
Greek term for recollection as a source of human knowledge. Socrates himself may have argued that recollection establishes mathematical truths independently of sensory experience. In the mature philosophy of Plato, however, our ability to recollect the immutable form is taken to provide direct evidence of the pre-existence of the human soul.

■ anagkh [anankê]
Greek word for the logical or causal necessity of anything that cannot be otherwise than as it is.

■ anarchism
belief that an ideal human society should have no organised government, often accompanied by a practical disregard for the authority of existing governments.

■ Anaxagoras of Clazomenae (500-428 BCE)
an ancient Greek philosopher who taught at Athens, leaving fragments of his philosophical work. Despite his rejection of a fundamental distinction between appearance and reality,

and adoption of an atomistic natural philosophy, Anaxagoras was the first philosopher in the Western tradition to draw a substantial distinction between inert and chaotic matter on one hand, while mind as an active principle and source of order on the other.

■ Anaximander (611-547 BCE)

pre-socratic philosopher. According to fragmentary reports from other philosophers, Anaximander speculated that all matter results from the distillation of hot, cold, dry, and wet elements from apeirwn an infinite, intelligent, living whole. Examination of fossil evidence persuaded Anaximander that living beings develop from simpler to more complex forms over time.

■ Anaximenes (c. 550 BCE)

pre-socratic philosopher. In fragmentary reports from other philosophers, Anaximenes is said to hold that condensation and evaporation of vapour or mist produces the physical world of earth, water, and fire.

■ ancestor-worship

cult of the dead or alive, drawn from the belief that the spirit or soul of an individual person survives physical decease.

■ andreia

the Greek term for bravery or courage.

■ anglicanism

teaching and practice of the Church of England, sister or daughter churches known collectively as the Anglican Communion.

■ angst

German word for anxiety or anguish produced by an acute awareness of the implications of human freedom.

■ **an hominem argument**
term is used for two kinds of argument. A fallacious argument whereby the premises merely attack a particular man while the conclusion purports to establish the falsity of a thesis he holds. The other kind of an argument is taking as its premise something that has been accepted by the other party but not perhaps by the arguer and deducing a consequence unacceptable to that other party.

■ **anima**
Latin term for wind, breath, life. Thus, for Descartes and other philosophers, the rational soul of any human being.

■ **animals**
many philosophers of the Western tradition have considered the relationship between human beings and other species of animals. Although some have been impressed with the obvious similarities in organic structure and behaviour, most have tried to draw a clear distinction between the two. Only recently few have taken seriously the extent of our moral obligations to fellow sentient beings.

■ **animal rights**
the ontological status accorded to non-human animals has obvious consequences for the morality of our willingness to use them for our own purposes.

■ **animism**
a belief that everything in the universe has some kind of soul or is a living being.

■ **Anselm of Canterbury**
British Benedictine theologian who devised the Ontological Argument for the existence of God.

■ **an sich**
1. element that states a prior condition in any conditional statement.

2. in a true material implication, the truth of its antecedent is incompatible with the falsity of its consequent.

■ anthropic principle

belief that the existence of human life entails certain features of the physical world. In a minimal form, this view merely points out that we would not be here to observe natural phenomena were they not compatible with our existence. Stronger versions of the anthropic principle, however, seem to rely upon the idealistic notion that the universe could not exist without intelligent observers.

■ anthropomorphism

attribution of human characteristics to non-human things. Thus, an anthropomorphic religion treats God as a personal being, and anthropomorphic natural theories may suppose that plants, animals, or the earth itself think and feel the same way that we do.

■ anthropopathism

a term coined by the writer and critic John Ruskin to designate the state of mind leading to what he called the 'pathetic fallacy'. This essentially means an emotional strain or a grief leading the poet to ascribe to nature the emotions of sympathy or cruelty.

■ anthroposophy

refers to an occult system which claims that the key to wisdom and to an understanding of the universe lies in man himself.

■ antichrist

this term simply means one who denies Christ. In extension, however, the term signifies a great force, filling the world with evil, whose defeat will lead to the Second Coming.

■ anticipations of experience

Kant's doctrine that all sensations have some intensive magnitude or degree. According to Kant we can anticipate the sensation, but not the magnitude or the degree of the same.

■ antilogism

a Greek term, meaning a method of checking on the validity of a syllogism.

antinomianism
view that ordinary moral laws are not applicable to Christians, whose lives, it is said, are governed solely by divine grace.

antinomy
a pair of equally defensible yet contradictory conclusions.

antithesis
reversal of an initial conviction. See **thesis / antithesis / synthesis.**

anxiety
according to many existentialist philosophers, the normal emotional response to the overwhelming responsibility entailed by human freedom.

apeirwn
Anaximander's Greek word for the boundless extent of the universe as undifferentiated matter. Although Plato made only scant reference to this notion of what is unlimited, the neo-platonic philosophy of Plotinus elevated it as the material principle of all change.

apodeictic
characteristic feature of any proposition that states what is necessary.

apodosis
a Greek term which means 'a giving back'.

apollinarianism
the christological doctrine that in Jesus the Logos assumed a human body, exercising the functions ordinarily performed by mind.

apologetics
a branch of theology that tries to justify a dogma by means of arguments addressed to reason. Apologetics is included in the Catholic and the orthodox systems of theology.

apology
refers to a form of discourse in defence of one's position. Among the most famous instances of such discourse one may cite Plato's Apology, giving Socrates' defence of his philosophic life and mission the entire movement of early Christian apologists and Cardinal Newman's Apologia pro Vita Sua, where he defends his philosophical and religious development, including his leaving the Anglican Church for Catholicism.

aporia
Greek term for a difficulty or a puzzle . Aristotle commonly used this term to signify a group of individuals.

a posteriori
depending upon or being justified by reference to sensory experience. **See: a priori / a posteriori.**

appearance / reality
distinction between the way things seem to be and the way they are. The merely apparent is often supposed to be internal, subjective, or temporal, but available for direct awareness, whereas the real is supposed to be external, objective, or eternal, but known only inferentially.

apperception
self-conscious awareness.

applied ethics
branch of ethics that considers the practical application of ethical principles to specific issues of social or personal concern.

a priori / a posteriori
distinction among judgements, propositions, concepts, ideas, arguments, or kinds of knowledge. In each case, the a priori is taken to be independent of sensory experience, which the a posteriori presupposes. An a priori argument is taken to reason deductively from abstract general premises, while an a posteriori argument relies upon specific information derived from sense perception. The necessary truth of an a priori proposition can be determined by reason alone, but the contingent truth of an a posteriori proposition can be discovered only by reference to some matter of fact.

arch
Greek term for beginning or ultimate principle.

Archimedes
Sicilian geometrician, who calculated an accurate value for π, demonstrated the relationship between the volume of spheres and cylinders, discovered methods for determining the centre of gravity of plane figures, and provided a foundation for the science of hydrostatics.

■ **arche**
a Greek term which signifies 'something in the beginning.'

■ **Archelaus of Athens**
a pupil of Anaxagoras and teacher of Socrates. His small contribution, to cosmology rather than philosophy, seems to have consisted in amending the system of Anaxagoras, using elements drawn from other predecessors.

■ **archetypes**
in Plato's philosophy, Ideas or Forms are considered to be the archetypes or prototypes. Such archetypes are original and immutable. They represent Being, while all other objects or things are mere copies of those ideas or forms. These objects or things represent the state of 'becoming'. In Berkeley's philosophy, those ideas, which potentially exist in the mind of God, are archetypes.

■ **architectonic**
term used to describe a philosophical system constructed according to a consistent plan.

■ **arête**
Greek word for unique excellence or skill of any sort. Socrates supposed that arête can be identified with knowledge of the good, but Plato distinguished four distinct virtues as crucial components of the perfect state or person. Aristotle maintained that moral arête is invariably found as the mean between vicious extremes.

■ **argument**
a collection of two or more propositions, all, but one, of which are the premises supposed to provide inferential support—either deductive or inductive—for the truth of the remaining one, the conclusion. The structure of arguments is the principal subject of logic.

argument form
general logical structure of an argument, considered apart from any of its specific content. In categorical logic, an argument form is any one of the 256 distinct varieties of categorical syllogism.

Aristotelian logic
traditional categorical logic, as developed originally in the works of Aristotle.

Aristotelianism
a tradition, dating from the mediaeval period, concerned with promoting and defending significant portions of the philosophy of Aristotle.

Aristotle
Greek philosopher who developed an observational and logical method for investigating the natural world.

artificial intelligence
scientific research aimed at building machines capable of performing a variety of functions as well as (or better than) human agents do. Although early efforts focussed on symbolic manipulation and linguistic representation, most now use the notion of parallel distributed processing for the construction of a quasi-neural network that recognises and associates patterns. The success of this discipline often gives rise to philosophical questions about whether purely physical systems can adequately support consciousness, perception and mind.

articles of faith
propositions concerning the interpretation of a religion, which have to be taken on faith.

■ artificial language
any non-natural language such as Esperanto or Ido. Natural languages are ordinary languages such as English, French, Chinese, Russian, etc.

■ asceticism
from the Greek askesis, which means 'self-denial'. An important theme of both Eastern and Western religion, that the body is to be denied, possibly mortified, to purify the soul in the process of salavation.

■ Asclepius
Greek God of medicine.

■ assent
make a judgement. For many philosophers of the modern period, it is the mental act of accepting the truth of a statement, whether or not one has adequate evidence for knowing it.

■ assertoric
a proposition stating that something actually is the case, rather than necessary or merely possible.

■ assertoric judgement
one of the three modes of judgement distinguished by Kant that assert something. The other two modes have been those of the problematic judgement and the Apodcictic judgement. The analysis of modality goes back at least to Aristotle.

■ association
associativity of both disjunction and conjunction can be demonstrated by truth-table analysis.

■ association of ideas
presumed regularities in the co-existence or succession of particular mental contents.

■ assumption
a proposition accepted without proof or evidence as the basis for some further conclusion.

■ ataraxia
a Greek term used by Pyrrho and Epicurus for tranquility, or the freedom from disturbance

and pain that characterises a balanced mind and constitutes its first step towards the achievement of pleasure

■ atheism
belief that God does not exist.

■ atomic proposition
also known as elementary proposition, it is a proposition in which there is no logical operator.

■ atomic sentence
a sentence that is logically simple.

■ atomism
belief that matter is composed of simple, indivisible, physical particles that are too tiny to be observed by human beings.

■ attribute
a property or a feature possessed by a substance. In the philosophical nomenclature employed by Aquinas and Descartes, attributes are commonly regarded as essential to the substances that have them.

■ Augustine
North African philosopher and theologian who blended the philosophy of Plato with Christianity but insisted nevertheless that faith holds an absolute priority over reason.

■ Austin, J. L.
English philosopher who developed a unique method of approaching philosophical issues, beginning with a painstakingly detailed analysis of the subtleties involved in the day-to-day uses of ordinary language.

■ authenticity
self-conscious appropriation of one's own existence and identity. According to Heidegger, such deliberate reflection about the goals and values of life is the only successful response to the experience of Angst without falling into self-deception.

■ authority, appeal to
informal fallacy of claiming that we ought to accept the truth of a proposition because of some personal feature of the individual who affirms it.

■ autonomy / heteronomy of the will
autonomous agents are self-legislating. They act accord-

ing to the categorical imperative of willing only what is universalisable as moral law. Heteronomous agents derive principles of action from outside themselves, by considering the objects or consequences of their choices or being influenced by the will of others.

■ Avernus

a deep lake near Puteoli, believed to be an entrance to the Underworld.

■ avowals

Gilbert Ryle used this term to denote first person utterances like 'I am in pain' to distinguish them from their third person counterparts like 'He is in pain'. Ryle felt that the third person statements are open to doubt, as one cannot introspect into the feelings of others while the first person statements are infallible.

■ axiology

branch of philosophy that studies judgements about values, including those of both aesthetics and ethics.

■ axiom

a proposition formally accepted without demonstration, proof, or evidence as one of the starting-points for the systematic derivation of an organised body of knowledge.

■ axiomatic method

method of formalising and studying a subject by using only the method of formal logic in order to derive the truths of the subject from a list of undefined terms and a list of axioms.

■ axiom of infinity

an axiom of set theory that asserts, in one form or an other, that there exists a set with infinitely many members.

■ Ayer, Alfred Jules (1910-1989)

English philosopher. After studying with members of the Vienna circle, Ayer published Language, Truth, and Logic (1936), an excellent statement of the central views of logical positivism, including the use of verifiability as a criterion of meaning, the rejection of metaphysics and theology as meaningless and an emotivist ethical theory. His later works include Foundations of Empirical Knowledge (1940), The Problem of Knowledge (1956), Logical Positivism (1966) and The Central Questions of Philosophy (1972).

■ Babbage, Charles (1792-1871)

English mathematician. A century before the development of electronic computers, Babbage invented a mechanical 'difference engine' for the calculation of arithmetical functions and set out plans for an 'analytical engine' whose operation would have included logarithmic and trigonometric functions as well. Babbage's interest in the practical conduct of business led to an extensive commentary on the inefficiency of common practices in The Economy of Machinery and Manufactures (1832), Comparative View of the Various Institutions for the Assurance of Lives and Reflections on the Decline of Science in England.

■ Bachelard, Gaston (1884-1962)

French philosopher of science and the author of Psychoanalyse du feu (Psychoanalysis of Fire) (1937), Le nouvel esprit scientifique (The New Scientific Spirit) (1934) and L'Actualitiè de l'histoire des sciences (History of Science) (1951). Rejecting both naive realism and absolute idealism, Bachelard maintained that scientific knowledge emerges from an imaginative interaction between the mind and experimental evidence. His emphasis on discontinuity in the progress of science anticipated portions of the work of Thomas Kuhn.

■ Bacon, Francis (Lord Verulam) (1561-1626)

English politician and philosopher. Bacon became Lord Chancellor of England in 1618, but was driven immediately from office under charges of official corruption. As an early empiricist, he rejected scholastic accounts of the natural world in favour of a new method for achieving knowledge, based exclusively on careful observation and cautious induction, which he described in The Advancement of Learning (1605) and Novum Organum (New Organon) (1620). Bacon warned that effective reasoning must be freed from the 'idolatrous'influence of personal interest, human nature, social conventions and academic philosophy. In The New Atlantis (1626), Bacon described the far-reaching social consequences of his epistemological programme. Bacon's Essays (1601) address the whole range of his philosophical and social interests.

■ Bacon, Roger (1214-1292)

English philosopher who translated many Aristotelian treatises from Arabic into Latin. Although passionately interested in alchemy and magic, Roger defended reliance upon mathematics and experimental methods for the improvement of human knowledge generally, and theological understanding in particular, in the Opus Maius (Greater Work) (1267) and On Experimental Science (1268). His novel educational doctrines were supposed to violate the condemnation of 1277 and much of Roger's later work, including the Compendium Studii Theologiae (1292) was suppressed.

■ bad faith

in the philosophy of Sartre, an effort to avoid anxiety by denying the full extent of one's own freedom. Bad faith, on this view, is an especially harmful variety of self-deception, since it forestalls authentic appropriation of responsibility for ourselves.

Baier, Annette (1929-)

American moral philosopher. From a thoughtful reading of Hume, Baier derives an ethical stance that emphasises the importance of membership within a moral community in A Progress of Sentiments: Reflections on Hume's Treatise (1991). In 'What Do Women Want in a Moral Theory?' (1983), she argues that the concept of trust provides a vital link between traditional (male) accounts of rational obligation and the equally traditional (female) 'ethics of love'. Her most recent publications include Moral Prejudices: Essays on Ethics (1994) and The Commons of the Mind.

Baier, Kurt (1917-)

American moral philosopher. In The Moral Point of View (1958), Baier argues that practical reasoning that takes into account both individual and social considerations is the appropriate method for deciding 'what is the best thing to do' in particular circumstances. Thus, we are moral because it is rational so to be, even when our private interests are outweighed by the welfare of others.

Bakunin, Mikhail Alexandrovich (1814-1876)

Russian philosopher and political anarchist. Author of Marxism, Freedom and the State (1872) and God and the State (1916). Bakunin participated in several European revolutionary movements in an effort to derive practical benefits from the theories of Marx and Proudhon. His philosophical writings emphasised the use of negative arguments as a dialectical method for defining creative results rather than relying upon pseudo-scientific theories of government.

Bayes, Thomas (1702-1761)

English clergyman and mathematician. 'Bayes theorem', first stated in his Essay towards solving a problem in the doctrine of chances (1764), proposes that evidence confirms the likelihood of an hypothesis only to the degree that the appearance of this evidence would be more probable with the assumption of the hypothesis than without it.

■ Bayle, Pierre (1647-1706)

French philosopher whose monumentally complex Dictionnaire historique et critique (Historical and Critical Dictionary) (1697) helped to promote the development of modern scepticism and greatly influenced the philosophy of Hume.

■ beauty

the characteristic feature of things that arouse pleasure or delight, especially to the senses of a human observer. Thus, 'beauty' is the most general term of aesthetic appreciation. Whether judgements about beauty are objective or subjective has been a matter of serious philosophical dispute.

■ Beauvoir, Simone de (1908-1986)

French existentialist philosopher and novelist, author of Le Deuxième Sexe (The Second Sex) (1949).

■ Bedeutung

Frege's German term for the reference of a concept.

■ begging the question (petitio principii)

circular reasoning. The 'informal fallacy' of (explicitly or implicitly) assuming the truth of the conclusion of an argument as one of the premises employed in an effort to demonstrate its truth. Example: 'Since firefighters must be strong men willing to face danger every day, it follows that no woman can be a firefighter.'

Although arguments of this sort are formally valid because it is impossible for their conclusions to be false if their premises are true, they fail to provide logical support for their conclusions, which have already been accepted without proof at the outset.

■ Begriff

German term for idea or concept.

behaviourism

belief that all mental phenomena can be explained by reference to publicly observable behaviour or dispositions to behave. Modern psychology, exemplified by Watson and Skinner, is founded on the methodological principle that only overt human conduct is available for objective study, including scientific prediction and confirmation. In a more radical metaphysical form, behaviourism may deny the reality of mental entities or processes, all of which are held to be reducible to physical things or events. Logical or linguistic behaviourism, like that of Gilbert Ryle, holds that assertions about mental events can always be analysed in behavioural terms. Contemporary functionalism is often regarded as a modest form of philosophical behaviourism.

belief (Gk. pistiV, Lat. fides)

affirmation of, or conviction regarding, the truth of a proposition, especially when one is not (yet) in possession of evidence adequate to justify a claim that the proposition is known with certainty.

Bentham, Jeremy (1748-1832)

English philosopher and political radical. In A Fragment on Government (1776) and An Introduction to the Principles of Morals and Legislation (1789), Bentham outlined an ethical system based on a purely hedonistic calculation of the utility of particular actions, with a view to the greatest happiness of all, a view later to be defended in modified form by Mill and others. Bentham supposed that consistent application of this principle in social and political life would resolve many difficulties in human conduct, using proportional but perfectly certain punishment, to render unacceptably painful to the prospective criminal any behaviour that would otherwise be likely to cause injury to others.

■ Berdyaev, Nicolai Alexandrovich (1874-1948)

Ukrainian philosopher who participated in the Revolution but was exiled to France in 1922. Distressed by totalitarian developments in communism, Berdyaev adopted a religious version of existentialism in which the themes of anxiety and authenticity are conveyed through the medium of traditional Christian mythology about sin and redemption. Vselenskost' i konfessio-nalism (Universality and Confessionalism) (1933) exemplifies the passionate individualism of this self-styled 'believing free-thinker', which seldom won institutional approval.

■ Bergmann, Gustav (1906-1987)

Austrian-American philosopher who employed the construction of an ideal language as a method for resolving ontological questions.

■ Bergson, Henri (1859-1941)

French philosopher. Rejecting sterile mechanistic accounts of the natural world, including those of Darwin and Spencer, Bergson developed an account that emphasised the subjective experience of time as the ground for human freedom in Essai sur les données immédiates de la conscience (Time and Free Will: An Essay on the Immediate Data of Consciousness) (1889), Matière et mémoire (Matter and Memory) (1896) and The Creative Mind: An Introduction to Metaphysics (1934). In L'Évolution créatrice (Creative Evolution) (1907), Bergson argued that thought, creativity, motion and evolution are all products of a creative impulse (Fr. élan vital) that emerges in opposition to material entropy. Bergson won the Nobel Prize for literature in 1927.

■ Berkeley, George (1685-1753)

British philosopher and bishop who used empiricist principles to defend an immaterialist philosophy.

Berlin, Isaiah (1909-1997)

Russian-British historian, diplomat and political philosopher. In Four Essays on Liberty (1969), Berlin drew an important distinction between the positive freedom to act and the negative freedom from interference in so acting. Societies that differ in their conceptions of liberty, Berlin argued, are likely to exhibit profoundly different social structures. Karl Marx: His Life and Environment (1939) and Historical Inevitability (1954) criticise the philosophy of Marx, with special treatment of his view of history.

best of all possible worlds

the qualitative character of reality, according to the Stoics, who supposed that all is as it should be. In a similar vein, Leibniz argued that an omnipotent and benevolent God would create nothing less, though Voltaire found the claim absurdly naive. In a venerable witticism, the optimist says brightly, 'This is the best of all possible worlds,' whereupon the pessimist sighs, 'I'm afraid you're right.'

Bewußtsein

German term for consciousness.

biconditional

the conjunction of two conditionals, the antecedent of each of which is the consequent of the other, that is, any statement of the form: 'P if and only if Q'. Although they may have other uses, all biconditionals involve at least the logical structure of material equivalence.

bivalence, principle of

supposition that every proposition must be either true or false. The status of this supposition is controversial, especially with respect to future propositions about human action. Thus, for example, if 'I will vacuum the carpet tomorrow.' were regarded as already true (or false) today, it would seem that I cannot freely choose whether or not to clean. Note the difference between bivalence and excluded middle.

■ Blanshard, Brand (1892-1987)

American philosopher and long-time professor at Yale University. In The Nature of Thought (1939), Blanshard defended absolute idealism and argued that causal necessity is a genuine feature of the natural world. According to Blanshard's Reason and Analysis, the philosophical methods of Anglo-American philosophers during the twentieth century were fundamentally misguided. He also rejected the prevalent non-cognitivism of twentieth-century ethicists, by defending a thoroughly naturalistic moral theory in Reason and Goodness (1962).

■ Bocardo

name given by mediaeval logicians to a categorical syllogism whose standard form has the mood and figure designated as OAO-3.

Example: Some local jails are not maximum-security prisons, but since all local jails are correctional institutions, it follows that some correctional institutions are not maximum-security prisons.

■ Boetius of Dacia (1230-1285)

Swedish Dominican philosopher. Doubts about personal immortality and the espousal of a fideistic account of the relation between faith and reason, during his service in Romania, resulted in the condemnation of his teachings, along with those of Siger of Brabant and the other radical Aristotelians.

■ Boethius, Anicius Manlius Severinus (480-524)

Roman logician. His Commentary on the Isagoge of Porphyry (itself a discussion of Aristotle's Categories) carefully distinguished Aristotelean essences from Platonic Forms, setting the basic terms employed in subsequent mediaeval discussion of the problem of universals. De consolatione philosophiae (The Consolation of Philosophy), written during the imprisonment that preceded his execution, considers the possibility of achieving human happiness despite the inescapable presence of evil, extols the benefits of reason even in the face of misfortune and bad advice and proposes a compatibalist account of human freedom in the face of divine foreknowledge.

■ Bohr, Niels Henrik David (1885-1962)

Danish physicist. Although best known for his contributions to atomic theory and quantum mechanics, Bohr also reflected on epistemological issues, defending a sophisticated variety of cultural relativism. Bohr won the Nobel Prize in Physics in 1922.

■ Bolzano, Bernard (1781-1848)

Austrian mathematician, theologian and philosopher. In opposition to the idealism of Kant and Hegel, Bolzano maintained that numbers, ideas and truths, all exist independently of the human beings who think about them. His Wissenschaftslehre (1837) and Grössenlehre (1850) offer a philosophical foundation for mathematics, employing a modern theory of classes to define the real numbers. Bolzano's work was a significant influence on that of Husserl, Frege, Lukasiewicz, and Tarski.

■ Bonaventure Giovanni di Fidanza (1221-1274)

Franciscan philosopher and theologian. Following Augustine, Bonaventure held that reason is valuable only in support of faith. Bonaventure's philosophy was predominantly neoplatonic, he accepted Aristotle's philosophical principles only when they could be used in service of his Christian aims, but argued against the eternal reality of the universe. In Itinerarium mentis in deum (The Journey of the Mind to God) (1259), he argued that human beings, as emanations of the deity, embody a footprint of the divine nature.

■ Boole, George (1815-1864)

British logician whose The Mathematical Analysis of Logic (1847) proposed the

'Boolean algebra' of propositional connectives representing negation and conjunction. An Investigation into the Laws of Thought (1859) further develops a symbolic system for the expression and evaluation of categorical syllogisms, understood as elements in the logic of classes.

■ Bordo, Susan (1947-)

American philosopher. In The Flight to Objectivity: Essays on Cartesianism and Culture (1987), she explores the masculinisation of thought in Cartesian modernism. Bordo's Unbearable Weight: Feminism, Western Culture, and the Body (1993) is a cultural exploration of the significance of social constructions of the human body. Similar themes are explored in Bordo's Twilight Zones: The Hidden Life of Cultural Images from Plato to O.J. (1997) and The Male Body: A New Look at Men in Public and in Private (1999).

■ Bosanquet, Bernard (1848-1923)

British philosopher who defended a modified version of Hegel's absolute idealism in Logic, or the Morphology of Knowledge (1888), The Principle of Individuality and Value (1912) and The Value and Destiny of the Individual (1914). According to Bosanquet, all contradictions are merely apparent and are wholly harmonised as part of the Absolute, a process said to account for the possibility of judgements about beauty in his History of Aesthetics (1892). Bosanquet further argued in The Philosophical Theory of the State (1899) that individual human beings are properly understood only in terms of their social and cultural efforts at transcendence.

■ Boundless, the (Gk. apeirwn [apeirôn])

the eternal, infinite, undifferentiated stuff, from which Anaximander believed the material world to be formed.

■ Bradley, Francis Herbert (1846-1924)

English philosopher and absolute idealist. His Ethical Studies (1876) criticised Mill's utilitarianism and defended an ethics of self-realisation, understood as the conquest of the bad self by the good. Bradley's metaphysical views, akin to those of Hegel, with a special emphasis on the internal relations of the Absolute, are developed at length in Appearance and Reality (1893) and defended in Essays on Truth and Reality (1914). Bradleian metaphysics became the primary target for the anti-idealistic polemics of Moore and Russell.

Brentano, Franz Clemens (1838-1917)

German philosopher and psychologist. An early phenomenologist, Brentano proposed the notion that intentionality is the mark of the mental, in Psychologie vom empirischen Standpunkt (Psychology from an Empirical Standpoint) (1874). He developed an associated theory of truth in Wahrheit und Evidenz (The True and the Evident) (1930) and applied phenomenological methods to ethical issues in Vom Ursprung sittlicher Erkenntnis (The Origin of Our Knowledge of Right and Wrong) (1889), defending a pluralistic view of objective intrinsic value.

Broad, Charlie Dunbar (1887-1971)

English philosopher. Although he criticised the extravagant speculation of absolute idealists like McTaggart in his Examination of McTaggart's Philosophy (1933, 1938), Broad was more willing than his contemporaries, Russell and Moore, to engage in metaphysical as well as epistemological theorising. The philosophy of mind, expressed in Scientific Thought (1923) and The Mind and its Place in Nature (1925), clearly defended the reality of physical and mental phenomena, including (notoriously) the possibility of genuine parapsychological phenomena.

Bruno, Giordano (1548-1600)

Italian philosopher of the Renaissance and follower of Nicolas of Cusa. An aposotate Dominican, Bruno tried to incorporate both Copernican astronomy and hermetic mysticism into an atomistic physics. His evident inclination towards pantheism and explicit identification of infinite matter as the eternal substance of the universe, in Dell' infinito, universo e mondi (On the Infinite Universe and Worlds) (1584), De Gli Eroici Furori (The Heroic Frenzies) (1585) and De immenso et innumerabilibus (1591), earned him the condemnation of the church, which expressed its displeasure by burning him at the stake in Rome.

■ Buber, Martin (1878-1965)

Austrian-Jewish theologian. In Ich und Du (I and Thou) (1922), Buber suggested that genuinely religious experiences must involve reciprocal intersubjective relations between persons rather than a merely objective apprehension of abstract reality. After emigrating to Israel Buber served as first President of the Academy of Science and Humanities.

■ bundle theory

belief that an object comprises only the features or properties it exhibits, without requiring the unifying presence of any underlying substance. Most notably, Hume supposed that the human self or mind is nothing more than a bundle of perceptions, linked to each other only by contingent associations.

■ Burke, Edmund (1729-1797)

Irish politician and philosopher. In the early A Philosophical Enquiry into the Origin of our Ideas of the Sublime and Beautiful (1757), Burke offered an analysis of aesthetic judgement that greatly influenced the work of Kant. Burke's Reflections on the Revolution in France (1790) includes an explicit criticism of the social contract theory, an extended appeal for the preservation of established social and political institutions, and the defence of a society ruled by respect for the rights and privileges revealed in traditional value-systems, including established religion.

Caird, Edward (1835-1908)

Scottish Hegelian philosopher. Caird was one of the first generation of 'British idealists', whose philosophical work was largely in reaction to the then-dominant empiricist and associationist views of Alexander Bain (1818-1903) and J.S. Mill. Best known for his studies of Kant — A Critical Account of the Philosophy of Kant (1877) and The Critical Philosophy of Immanuel Kant (1889)— and Hegel — Hegel (1883), Caird also exercised a strong influence on later idealists such as John Watson and Bernard Bosanquet, particularly concerning the development of an 'evolutionary' account of religion.

Cambridge Platonists

an influential group of seventeenth-century English philosophers and latitudinarian theologians, who rejected the tenets of (Oxford-taught) scholasticism, in favour of an eclectic rationalism that employed a neo-platonic metaphysics and placed great emphasis on the role of innate ideas in the acquisition of worthwhile knowledge of reality, while opposing the mechanism of the new science and the atheism, to which they feared it might lead. Prominent members of the group included Cudworth, Cumberland, Glanvill, More, Conway and Norris.

Camenes

name given by mediaeval logicians to a categorical syllogism whose standard form is AEE-4. Example: All first-degree murders are premeditated homicides, but no premeditated homicides are actions performed in self-defence, so it follows that no actions performed in self-defence are first-degree murders.

Camestres

name given by mediaeval logicians to any categorical syllogism whose standard form may be designated as AEE-2. Example: All terriers are dogs, while no cats are dogs, so no cats are terriers.

■ Camus, Albert (1913-1960)

French-Algerian journalist and novelist. Camus explored the practical consequences of existentialist philosophy in his novels, L'Étranger (The Stranger) (1942), La Peste (The Plague) (1947), L'Homme Révolté (The Rebel) (1951) and La Chute (The Fall) (1956). His essay Le Mythe de Sisyphe (Essai sur l'absurde) (The Myth of Sisyphus) (1943) describes the inherent absurdity of human life, a profound meaninglessness that can be mitigated only by moral integrity and social solidarity. Camus was awarded the Nobel Prize in 1957 and died in an automobile accident three years later.

■ Cantor, Georg Ferdinand Ludwig Philipp (1845-1918)

German mathematician. Cantor developed modern set theory as the foundation for all of mathematics and used the 'diagonal proof' to demonstrate that lines, planes and spaces must all contain a non-denumerable infinity of points. That is, they cannot be counted in a one-to-one correspondence with the rational numbers. The reality of transfinite quantities within the set of real numbers leads, in turn to 'Cantor's paradox'—that every set has more subsets than members, so that there can be no set of all sets.

■ Carneades (214-129 B.C.E.)

Greek philosopher. As leader of the Academy, Carneades advocated a moderate scepticism, which permitted the qualified assertion of probable judgements. In his own time, Carneades was famous for the ability to develop convincing arguments on both sides of any philosophical dispute.

■ Carroll, Lewis (Charles Lutwidge Dodgson) (1832-1898)

English logician, mathematician, and author. Carroll's fascination with logical and philosophical puzzles is apparent in the popular books Alice's Adventures in Wonderland (1865) and Through the Looking Glass (1876), as well as in the more technical Games of Logic (1887) and Symbolic Logic (1893). The philosophical paper on 'What the Tortoise said to Achilles' (1895) raised a significant issue about the legitimacy of reiterated demands for epistemological justification.

■ Cartesianism

school of seventeenth-century thinkers who pursued the philosophical aims of Descartes. Prominent examples include Cordemoy, Geulincx, Malebranche, Pascal, Régis and Rohault. The Cartesians tried to develop a comprehensive science of nature and to resolve the problems about mind-body interaction raised by Descartes's dualism.

■ Cassirer, Ernst (1874-1945)

German neo-Kantian philosopher who supposed that the fundamental categories of human thought are genuinely a priori, yet develop historically. In his massive Die Philosophie der symbolischen Formen (The Philosophy of Symbolic Forms) (1929), Cassirer suggested that these basic concepts are most clearly revealed in the cultural symbols of language, science and mythology.

■ casuistry

approach to ethics that begins by examining a series of concrete cases, rather than by trying to deduce the consequences of a moral rule. Although Pascal criticised this method for the excessive, misleading or harmful cleverness with which it was practised in his day, it remains a common tool for applied ethics in a theological vein.

■ categorical / hypothetical imperative

in the moral philosophy of Kant, a distinction between ways in which the will may be obliged. A hypothetical imperative (of the form, 'If you want X, then do A.') is always conditioned on something else, but a categorical imperative (of the form 'Do A.') is absolute and universal. Moral action for Kant always follows from the categorical imperative, 'Act only according to that maxim whereby you can at the same time will that it become a universal law'.

■ categorical logic

the traditional interpretation of the logic of classes developed by Aristotle and the mediaeval logicians.

■ categorical proposition

a statement of the relationship between two classes, each of which is designated by a categorical term. Within each proposition, the subject term occurs before the copula and the predicate term after. There are only four forms of categorical proposition, distinguished by their quantity and quality.

■ categorical syllogism

a logical argument consisting of exactly three categorical propositions, two premises and the conclusion, with a total of exactly three categorical terms, each used in only two of the propositions.

■ categorical term

a word or phrase that designates a class. Each categorical term divides the world into two parts: the original class and its complement, the things to which the term applies and those to which it does not.

■ category (Gk. kathgoria [katêgoria])

predicate, hence, a fundamental class of things in our conceptual framework. In Aristotle's logic specifically, the categories are the ten general modes of being (substance, quantity, quality, relation, place, time, position, possession, doing and undergoing) by reference to which any individual thing may be described. Following the lead of stoic thought, mediaeval logicians commonly employed only the first four of these ten, but allowed for additional, syncategorematic terms that belonged to none of them. Kant employed a schematised table of a dozen categories as the basis for our understanding of the phenomenal realm. Gilbert Ryle used the term much more broadly, warning of the category mistakes that occur when we fail to respect the unique features of kinds of things.

category mistake
confusion in the attribution of properties or the classification of things. Thus, to suppose that sleep is furious or that a city is nothing more than its buildings is to commit a category mistake. Ryle maintained that Cartesian dualism arises from the implicit occurrence of just such an error, the supposition that the origins of human behaviour must reside in an immaterial substance.

catharsis (Gk. kaqarsiV [katharsis])
cleansing from guilt or defilement. Hence, in Aristotle, the elimination of destructive emotions through appreciation of an aesthetic experience. The notion here is that vicariously experiencing strong feelings renders us less likely to be overcome by them in our own lives.

cause / effect (Ger. Ursache / Wirkung)
distinction between the events involved in a causal relationship, where the occurrence of one (the cause) is supposed to bring about or produce an occurrence of the other (the effect). Although the correct analysis of causation is a matter of great dispute, Hume offered a significant criticism of our inclination, to infer a necessary connection from mere regularity and Mill proposed a set of methods for recognising the presence of causal relationships. Contemporary philosophers often suppose that a causal relationship is best expressed in the counterfactual statement that if the cause had not occurred, then the effect would not have occurred either.

causes, the four (Gk. aitia [aitia])
Aristotle's distinction in the Physics among four answers to the question of why something is:
the material cause is the stuff from which the thing is made

the formal cause is the pattern or structure it has.
the efficient cause is the agent that imposed this form on that matter.
the final cause is the purpose for the thing.
Thus, for example, the material cause of this chair is the wood out of which it is made, the formal cause is the shape into which it was fashioned, the efficient cause was the carpenter by whom the chair was made and the final cause is the sitting for the sake of which it was designed. In the case of living beings, Aristotle supposed, the soul is the formal, efficient and final cause, and the body is only the material cause.

■ Cavendish, Margaret (1623-1673)

English philosopher and playwright. Cavendish criticised the natural philosophy of both Hobbes and Descartes, in Philosophical Letters (1664), and that of Boyle, in Observations upon Experimental Philosophy (1666). Her own view, developed fully in The Grounds of Natural Philosophy (1668), was materialist but not mechanistic, supposing that all matter is imbued with soul. In A True Relation of my Birth, Breeding, and Life (1656), Cavendish commented upon the place of women in seventeenth-century society.

■ Celarent

name given by mediaeval logicians to any categorical syllogism whose standard form may be designated as EAE-1. Example: No cold-blooded animals are furry pets, even though all reptiles are cold-blooded animals, therefore, no reptiles are furry pets.

■ Cesare

name given by mediaeval logicians to a categorical syllogism whose standard form is EAE-2. Example: Since no truly peaceful nations are places where basic human rights are inadequately defended, while all countries torn by ethnic strife are places where basic human rights are inadequately defended, it follows that no countries torn by ethnic strife are truly peaceful nations.

chain of being

belief that existing things can be hierarchically ordered, from least to greatest, in an unbroken series from inanimate particles of matter to the deity. A. O. Lovejoy traced this concrete application of the principle of plenitude from ancient Greek thought through neo-platonism to its influence on early twentieth-century idealism.

Chomsky, Noam Avram (1928-)

American linguist and philosopher, author of Syntatactic Structures (1957), Cartesian Linguistics (A chapter in the history of rationalist thought) (1966), Language and Mind (1968) and Knowledge of Language (1986). In opposition to prevalent behaviourism, Chomsky's psycholinguistic approach holds that competence in the use of language reveals innate possession of universal generative grammatical structures that cannot be acquired simply by empirical evidence. Chomsky has also been an outspoken and thoughtful critic of American foreign policy since the 1960s, in such books as American Power and the New Mandarins (1969), Necessary Illusions (1989) and Deterring Democracy (1992).

Chrysippus (280-207 B.C.E.)

primary author of the stoic philosophy. Although none of his many writings survived antiquity, Chrysippus reportedly made significant contributions to the development of logic and ethics. He is generally credited with invention of the propositional calculus and eloquent expression of the doctrine of eternal return.

circularity

reasoning that improperly assumes the truth of what is at issue. A circular argument implicitly employs its own conclusion as a premise. A circular definition defines an expression in terms of itself. The problem is that circular reasoning, however accurate, is bound to be uninformative.

■ class

any collection or group of things, whether natural or arbitrary. In traditional logic, classes are designated by categorical terms.

■ clear and distinct

features of ideas considered as mental entities, without regard for their external relation to objects they are supposed to represent. An idea is clear if its content is precise and detailed, otherwise, it is obscure. An idea is distinct if it can be distinguished from any other idea, confused if it cannot. (Although the two notions are formally distinct, they are commonly supposed to coincide, on the grounds that clarity is a necessary and sufficient condition for distinctness.) Descartes held that the clarity and distinctness of our ideas is a criterion for the truth of what we believe.

■ cogito ergo sum (Fr. je pense, donc je suis)

'I think, therefore I am.' Latin translation of the first truth that Descartes believed to escape his radical method of doubt.

■ cognition

the portion of human experience comprising thought, knowledge, belief and inference (as opposed to sensation, volition or feeling).

■ cognitive science

interdisciplinary effort to study and explain the processes of human thought as a system of symbol manipulation or computational rules.

■ coherence theory of truth

belief that a proposition is true to the extent that it agrees with other true propositions. In contrast with the correspondence theory's emphasis on an independent reality, this view supposes that reliable beliefs constitute an inter-related system, each element of which entails every other. Thus, such idealists as Bradley, Bosanquet and Blanshard, all defended versions of the coherence theory.

■ communism

shared possession of property by all members of a society. Hence, the political movement, fostered by Marx and Engels, that encourages formation of a proletarian state for the purpose of overcoming the class-structures and alienation of labour that characterise capitalistic societies.

■ commutation (Comm.)

a rule of replacement of the forms:

(p Ú q) ° (q Ú p).

(p ·q) ° (q ·p).

Example: 'Either Spot is brown or Tabby is white.' is equivalent to 'Either Tabby is white or Spot is brown.' Although trivial in ordinary language, the commutativity of disjunction and conjunction is a significant feature of the propositional calculus.

■ compatibilism

belief that the causal determination of human conduct is consistent with the freedom required for responsible moral agency.

■ complement

the class of all and only those things that are not included in the class designated by a categorical term. Thus, for example, things that go bump in the night is the complement of things that don't go bump in the night and vice versa.

■ completeness

a feature of formal systems whose axioms or rules of inference are adequate for the demonstration of every true proposition or for the justification of every valid argument. Thus, the addition of any unprovable formula to a complete system necessarily results in a contradiction. The propositional calculus is complete in this sense, but higher-order versions of quantification theory are not.

■ complex question

the informal fallacy of framing an issue as if it involved genuine alternatives, while implicitly assuming the truth of the desired conclusion. Example: 'Do you expect Peter to speak for thirty minutes or fifty? In either case, you

acknowledge that he will be long-winded.'
Denying the presumption that lies behind both alternatives (in this case, that Peter will speak for at least thirty minutes) would eliminate the supposed evidence that the conclusion is true.

■ composition, fallacy of
the informal fallacy of attributing some feature of the members of a collection to the collection itself or reasoning from part to whole. Example: 'Each of the elements in this compound (NaCl) is poisonous to human beings, therefore, this compound is itself poisonous to human beings.'

■ concept
any abstract notion or idea, by virtue of which we apply general terms to things.

■ conceptualism
solution to the problem of universals. According to Abelard, general terms are applied to individual things by reference to abstract ideas or concepts.

■ conclusion
a proposition whose truth has been inferred on the basis of other propositions assembled with it in a logical argument.

■ Concomitant Variation, Method of
one of Mill's Methods. If an antecedent circumstance is observed to change proportionally with the occurrence of a phenomenon, it is probably the cause of that phenomenon. Example: 'The more coffee I drink, the more difficult it is to fall asleep at night. Therefore, drinking coffee may be a cause of my insomnia.'

■ conditional
any statement of the form: 'If (antecedent), then (consequent).' Although conditionals may have several uses in ordinary language, all share at least the truth-functional structure of material implication.

■ confirmation
the relationship between empirical evidence and the scientific hypothesis it is used to support. Although abductive

reasoning can provide only partial or incomplete support for such hypothesis, their falsification by contradictory evidence can be absolute. Hempel pointed out a systematic paradox regarding the nature of confirming instances.

■ **conjunction**

a compound statement that is true just whenever both of its component statements (the conjuncts) are true.

p	q	p · q
T	T	T
T	F	F
F	T	F
F	F	F

Conjunctions are symbolised here in the form: p · q

■ **connective**

a logical symbol used to make compound statements out of simpler component statements. The truth-functional connectives used here include:

~ for negation

· for conjunction

Ú for disjunction

É for implication

º for equivalence.

■ **connotation**

the associative meaning of a term, including especially those features in virtue of which the term is properly applied.

■ **conscience**

inner awareness of the difference between right and wrong in one's own actions, usually understood as a divinely-inspired moral sense. Although Aquinas noted that an individual conscience may err, Butler held that it is the fundamental motive for good conduct.

■ **consciousness (Ger. Bewußtsein)**

the subjective phenomenon of self-awareness that normally accompanies human experience. Correct analysis of consciousness is a central goal in the philosophy of mind.

■ **consequent**

the element of a conditional statement that states its outcome or result. For example, 'You'll see me tomorrow' is the consequent of both:

'If you come by the office, then you'll see me tomorrow.' and 'You'll see me tomorrow, unless I see you first.'

■ **consequentialism**

any normative theory holding that human actions derive their moral worth solely from the outcomes or results that they produce. Utilitarianism is a consequentialist theory that typically identifies happiness or pleasure as the favoured consequence. One of the difficulties inherent in the practical application of any such theory is our notoriously feeble ability (or willingness), to predict accurately what consequences our own actions will produce.

■ **consistency**

feature of any formal system from whose axioms no direct contradiction follows. The customary proof of consistency is to show that there is at least one interpretation of the system upon which all of its axioms are true.

■ **constant**

in a system of formal logic, any symbol that, unlike a variable, specifically designates an item. Thus, the propositional calculus employs statement constants, while quantification theory makes use of both individual and predicate constants.

■ **Constructive Dilemma (C.D.)**

a rule of inference of the form:

(p É q) ·(r É s).
p Ú r.
q Ú s.

Example: 'If it's sunny tomorrow we'll have a picnic and if it rains we'll go bowling. But either it will be sunny or it will rain tomorrow. Therefore, either we'll have a picnic or we'll go bowling.'
The reliability of this pattern of reasoning is established by a truth-table.

■ **continence/incontinence**

distinction between modes of human action in the ethics of Aristotle. A continent agent is able to carry out actions that conform to th0e demands of reason, while an incontinent agent is overcome by desire and said to suffer from weakness of the will.

■ contingent

the status of a proposition that could, depending upon the circumstances, be either true or false. A compound statement in the propositional calculus is contingent if its truth depends upon that of its simpler components.

■ contradiction

a logical falsehood. A statement which, by virtue of its form, cannot be used to make a true assertion. For example: 'Sugar is sweet and sugar is not sweet.'

■ contradictories

a pair of categorical propositions, each of which is true if and only if the other is false. In the traditional square of opposition, an A proposition and its corresponding O are contradictories, as are an E proposition and its corresponding I. Thus, for example: 'All dogs are mammals and Some dogs are not mammals' are contradictories, as are 'No fish are tuna and Some fish are tuna'.

■ contraposition

the reciprocal relationship between two categorical propositions of the same form, such that the subject term of each is the complement of the predicate term of the other. Contraposition is a valid immediate inference for both A and O propositions. Thus, for example: 'All voters are citizens and All non-citizens are non-voters' and 'Some ants are not biters and Some non-biters are not non-ants' are legitimate cases of contraposition.

■ contraries

a pair of categorical propositions which (provided that we assume existential import) cannot both be true, but can both be false. In the traditional square of opposition, an A proposition and its corresponding E are contraries. Thus, for example: All cars are green and No cars are green are contraries.

■ conventionalism

belief that judgements of a specific sort are grounded only on (explicit or implicit) agreements in human society, rather than by reference to external reality. Although this view is commonly held with respect to the rules of grammar and the principles of etiquette, its application to the propositions of law, ethics, science, mathematics and logic is more controversial.

■ converse accident (Lat. a dicto secundum quid ad dictum simpliciter)
the informal fallacy of using exceptional specific cases as the basis for a general rule, omitting reference to their qualifying features. Example: 'It rained on my birthday this year and it rained on my birthday last year. Therefore, it always rains on my birthday.'

■ conversion
the reciprocal relationship between two categorical propositions of the same form, such that the subject term of each is the predicate term of the other. Conversion is a valid immediate inference for both E and I propositions. Thus, for example: 'No snakes are mammals and No mammals are snakes', like 'Some carnivores are birds and Some birds are carnivores' are each the converse of the other.

■ corpuscularianism
seventeenth century physical theory that supposed all matter to be composed of minute particles. Corpuscularians included Gassendi, Boyle, and Locke.

■ correspondence theory of truth
belief that a proposition is true when it conforms with some fact or state of affairs. While this theory properly emphasises the notion that propositions are true when they correspond to reality, its proponents often have difficulty explaining what facts are and how propositions are related to them.

■ cosmological argument
an attempt to prove the existence of God by appeal to contingent facts about the world. The first of Aquinas's five ways (borrowed from Aristotle's Metaphysics) begins from the fact that something is in motion: since ev-

erything that moves must be moved by another but the series of prior movers cannot extend infinitely, there must be a first mover (which is God). The second and third of the five ways begin from efficient causation and the existence of contingent beings.

■ counter-example

a particular instance that demonstrates the falsity of a general claim. Thus, for example, the fact that Don DeLillo is clean-shaven, is a counter-example to the claim that all great American novelists have beards.

■ counterfactual

a conditional statement whose antecedent is known (or, at least, believed) to be contrary to fact. Thus, for example, 'If George W. Bush had been born in Idaho, then he would never have become President.' Unlike material implications, counterfactuals are not made true by the falsity of their antecedents. Although they are not truth-functional statements, counterfactuals may be significant for the analysis of scientific hypothesis.

■ courage (Gk. andreia [andreia])

willingness to take reasonable risks in pursuit of a worthwhile goal. According to Plato, courage is vital for both social and personal embodiments of virtue.

■ criterion

a standard by means of which the features of things are judged. Possession of appropriate criteria necessarily constitutes adequate evidence for our attribution of the feature in question. Thus, as Wittgenstein noted, for example, observation of writhing and groaning are criteria for our belief that someone is in pain.

■ critical theory

the theoretical approach of the Frankfurt School of social philosophers. Relying on the work of Hegel and Marx, they tried to exhibit dialectically, the contradictions imposed upon modern human beings by varieties of social organisation that abuse formal rationality, in order to deny power to classes of citizens. Rejecting the detached insularity of traditional efforts at objectivity, critical theorists of any sort generally hope that their explanation of the causes of oppression will result in practical efforts to eliminate it.

■ **cynicism**

belief (expressed by Diogenes) that the entire point of human life is the satisfaction of our most basic natural needs, without any respect for social conventions. Thus, the Cynics practised self-discipline, in order to avoid the unhappiness that invariably results from any effort to pursue artificial obligations.

■ **Darii**

name given by mediaeval logicians to any categorical syllogism whose standard form may be designated as AII-1. Example: All logicians are philosophers and some serious scholars are logicians, so some serious scholars are philosophers.

■ **Dasein**

Heidegger's German term for 'Being there', the kind of existence that self-conscious human beings uniquely possess.

■ **Datisi**

name given by medieval logicians to a categorical syllogism with the standard form AII-3. Example: Since all bookstores are places that sell popular novels and some bookstores are coffee shops, it follows that some coffee shops are places that sell popular novels.

■ **decision procedure**

an algorithm by means of which to establish, in a finite number of steps, whether a statement form is tautologous or whether an argument form is valid. Drawing Venn diagrams provides a decision procedure for a modern interpretation of categorical logic and truth-tables give a decision procedure for the propositional calculus, but there is no decision procedure for quantification theory.

■ deconstruction
interpretive method that denies the priority or privilege of any single reading of a text (even if guided by the intentions of its author) and tries to show that the text is incoherent because its own key terms can be understood only in relation to their suppressed opposites.

■ Dedekind, J. W. Richard (1831-1916)
German mathematician who showed that every real number can be defined by reference to a 'cut' or division between sets of rational numbers. Dedekind also identified as axiomatic foundations of arithmetic which later became known as the Peano postulates.

■ de dicto / de re
distinction between ways of understanding the logical necessity or truth of statements, either in terms 'of what is said' (de dicto) or in terms 'of the thing' (de re). Someone who does not know that the morning star is the planet Venus, for example, could believe the truth, de dicto, of the proposition, 'The morning star is larger than Venus', even though no one would believe de re that Venus is larger than itself.

■ deduction / induction
distinction in logic between types of reasoning, arguments or inferences. In a deductive argument, the truth of the premises is supposed to guarantee the truth of the conclusion. In an inductive argument, the truth of the premises merely makes it probable that the conclusion is true.

■ de facto / de jure
distinction between the grounds for a condition that merely happens to obtain (de facto) and one that holds as a matter of right or law (de jure). The maximum speed at which an automobile may lawfully travel on the highway is 70 m.p.h. de jure, but the de facto speed limit on a busy afternoon is only about 50 m.p.h.

■ definite description
an expression that claims to refer to the single being that

possesses some unique feature. Russell showed nearly a century ago that the proper analysis of such expressions, as the joint assertion of several distinct propositions, resolves a number of otherwise troubling difficulties.

■ definition

an explanation of the meaning of a word. The five major kinds of definition (distinguished by the functions they may be used to perform) include: stipulative, lexical, precising, theoretical and persuasive.

■ deism

belief in God based entirely on reason, without any reference to faith, revelation or institutional religion. During the seventeenth and eighteenth centuries, advances in the natural sciences often fostered confidence that the regularity of nature reflects the benevolence of a divine providence. This confidence, together with a widespread distrust of the church, made deism a popular view in England and on the continent. Thus, in distinct ways, Toland, Lord Herbert, Paine, Rousseau, and Voltaire were all deists.

■ de jure

as a matter of law, not merely as a matter of fact. See **de facto / de jure.**

■ Democritus (460-370 BCE)

pre-socratic Greek philosopher. As the originator of classical atomism, Democritus maintained in opposition to the Eleatics that the universe comprises a plurality of distinct entities that really do move. The haphazard collisions of these individually indestructible atoms, he believed, account for the formation and dissolution of all observable things. Long before its appropriation by Epicurus, this doctrine produced an attitude towards human life that earned Democritus a reputation as 'the laughing philosopher'.

■ De Morgan's Theorems (De M.)

a rule of replacement of the forms:

~ (p · q) º (~ p Ú ~ q).
~ (p Ú q) º(~ p · ~ q).
Example: 'It is not the case that I am both bald and fat' is equivalent to 'Either I am not bald or I am not fat.' Truth-table analysis demonstrates the reliability of these logical relationships, as does a set-theoretical proof.

■ denotation / connotation

Mill's distinction between the things to which a term refers (its denotation) and the meaning of the term (its connotation). In modern logic, this distinction is often assimilated to the distinction between the extension and intension of an expression.

■ deontology

study of moral necessity, duty or obligation. A deontological normative theory holds that moral worth is an intrinsic feature of human actions, determined by formal rules of conduct. Thus, deontologists like Kant suppose that moral obligation rests solely upon duty, without requiring any reference to the practical consequences that dutiful actions may happen to have.

■ de re

of the thing, not of what is said. See **de dicto/de re**.

■ Derrida, Jacques (1930-).

French philosopher and leader of the deconstructionist movement. From the work of Husserl and Heidegger, Derrida derives the view that meaning emerges only provisionally, from an endless process of re-interpretation based on the interaction between reader and text. In La Voix et le phénoméne (Speech and Phenomena) (1967), L'écriture et la différance (Writing and Difference) (1967), De la Grammatologie (Of Grammatology) (1967) and La Dissémination (Dissemination) (1972), Derrida argues that all dichotomies between subject and object or appearance and reality are ultimately untenable.

■ Descartes, René (1596-1650)

French philosopher. Descartes's efforts to achieve certainty in the face of scepticism mark the origins of modern epistemology.

■ **descriptive ethics**
branch of ethics that non-judgementally examines the moral tenets of a particular society or tradition, analysing the logical relations among them and observing the extent of their application in practice.

■ **design, argument from**
belief that the operation of the universe evidences its providential origin.

■ **determinable / determinate**
relative terms for general predicates and particular instances that are not (like the species of a common genus) distinguishable by differentiae. Thus, for example, 'red', 'yellow', 'orange' and 'maroon' are all determinates of the determinable 'colour'.

■ **determinism**
belief that, since each momentary state of the world entails all of its future states, it must be possible (in principle) to offer a causal explanation for everything that happens. When applied to human behaviour, determinism is sometimes supposed to be incompatible with the freedom required for moral responsibility. The most extreme variety of determinism in this context is fatalism.

■ **Dewey, John (1859-1952)**
American philosopher and educator. During his long career, Dewey applied the principles of pragmatism not only to abstract philosophical issues but also to practical concerns, including the promotion of teaching as a profession.

■ **d'Holbach, Paul-Henri-Dietrich (1723-1789)**
French philosopher. Even among fellow Encyclopedists,

d'Holbach was noted for his vigorous materialism and the virulence of his atheistic attacks on revealed religion and deism in Le Christianisme dévoilé (Christianity Unmasked) (1761) and Système de la nature (The System of Nature) (1770).

dialectic (Gk. dialektikh [dialektikê])

process of thinking by means of dialogue, discussion, debate or argument. In ancient Greece, the term was used literally. Parmenides and the other Eleatics used such methods to defend paradoxical claims about the natural world. Dialectic is questioning and conversation for Socrates, but Plato regarded it as a systematic method for studying the Forms of suprasensible reality. Although he frequently employed dialectical methods in his own writing, Aristotle maintained that it is inferior to the careful logical reasoning that aims at theoretical knowledge.

German philosophers of the modern era applied the term 'dialectic' only to more narrowly-defined patterns of thinking. Thus, Kant's 'Transcendental Dialectic' is an attempt to show the general futility of abstract metaphysical speculation, but dialectic is, for Hegel, the fundamental process of development, in both thought and reality, from thesis to antithesis to synthesis.

dialectical materialism

philosophical doctrine expounded by Engels and Marx. By emphasising the independent reality of matter and the primary value of the natural world, they rejected the idealism of Hegel. But they fully accepted his notion of dialectic as an inexorable process of development in thought, nature and history.

dianoia [diánoia]

Greek term used by Plato to signify understanding or intellectual activity as a discursive process, in contrast with the immediate apprehension characteristic of nohsiV [nóêsis]. In the taxonomy of Aristotle, dianoia includes both the theoretical episthmh [epistêmê] and the more practical tecnh [technê].

■ Diderot, Denis (1713-1784)

French philosopher who edited the Encyclopédie. Diderot promoted Locke's thought in France through his Pensées sur l'interprétation de la nature (1746) and Lettre sur le aveugles (Essay on Blindness) (1749). In his later years, Diderot wrote essays and plays expressing favoured Enlightenment themes, including atheism and social contract theory.

■ difference, method of

one of Mill's methods for discovering causal relationships. If an antecedent circumstance is present only on those occasions when a phenomenon occurs, it may be inferred to be the cause of that phenomenon.

■ dikh (díkê)

Greek term for legal compensation or justice, the corresponding human virtue of being just is dikaiwsunh (dikaiôsunê). According to Plato, justice in this sense is best exemplified by harmonious relations in the ideal state. Aristotle, on the other hand, focussed primarily upon the equitable distribution of goods in a properly run city.

■ dilemma

a difficult choice between equally undesirable alternatives. In a disadvantageous rhetorical position, one is said to be impaled on the horns of a dilemma, but logicians employ Constructive Dilemma as a rule of inference.

■ Dimaris

name given by mediaeval logicians to any categorical syllogism whose standard form is IAI-4. Example: Some beloved household pets are golden retrievers and since all golden retrievers are dogs, it must follow that some dogs are beloved household pets.

■ Ding an sich

German phrase for thing in itself.

■ Diogenes (400-325 BCE)

Greek philosopher. As one of the original Cynics, Diogenes

both preached and practised a life of complete self-sufficiency, utter simplicity and total disregard for the conventional morality of what he took to be a corrupt human society. Diogenes was the teacher of Zeno of Citium.

■ **direct realism**

theory of perception, according to which we perceive material objects directly, without the mediation of ideas or sensory representations. Although it is also called 'naïve' realism, this view often requires a sophisticated defence, especially in its attempts to account for the occurrence of hallucinations and perceptual error.

■ **directive use of language**

communication that aims to bring about or to forestall the performance of some action. Example: 'Don't forget to take out the trash.'

■ **Disamis**

name given by mediaeval logicians to a categorical syllogism whose standard form may be designated as IAI-3. Example: Some nutritious dinners are vegetarian delights and all nutritious dinners are well-rounded meals, so some well-rounded meals are vegetarian delights.

■ **disjunction**

p	q	p Ú q
T	T	T
T	F	T
F	T	T
F	F	F

A compound statement that is true whenever either one or both of its component statements (the disjuncts) are true. Disjunctions are symbolised here in the form:

p Ú q

Example: 'Either the switch is off or the bulb is burned out.'

■ **disposition**

a tendency or propensity to respond in specific ways to particular circumstances. Things are commonly supposed to have dispositional features only in virtue of their possession of intrinsic or non-dispositional properties. Thus, for example, sugar is soluble in water (even when it is not in water) because of its chemical composition. Ryle maintained that mental states can be wholly analysed as dispositions of human bodies.

■ distribution of terms

a feature that categorical terms come to have by virtue of their use in a specific categorical proposition. The term is distributed if the proposition refers to every member of the class it designates, undistributed if it does not. Thus, the subject term is distributed in all and only universal propositions, while the predicate term is distributed in all and only negative propositions.

■ Distribution (Dist.)

a rule of replacement of the forms:

[p ·(q Ú r)] ° [(p ·q) Ú (p ·r)]

[p Ú (q ·r)] ° [(p Ú q) ·(p Ú r)]

Example: 'Paul is tall and so is either Susan or James' is equivalent to 'Either Paul and Susan are tall or Paul and James are'. The logical relationship between pairs of this sort may be demonstrated by the construction of a truth-table.

■ division, fallacy of

the informal fallacy of attributing some feature of a collection to the members of that collection individually or reasoning from whole to part.

■ double aspect theory

belief that mental properties and events on the one hand and physical properties and events on the other hand, are irreducibly distinct features or aspects of one and the same thing that exhibits them both. Spinoza, for example, maintained that thought and extension are distinct attributes of the one existing substance that is 'God or Nature'.

■ Double Negation (D.N.)

a rule of replacement of the form:

p ° ~ ~ p

Example: 'Alan is clever' is equivalent to 'It is not the case that Alan is not clever'. Although trivial in ordinary language, this rule is vital for the completeness of the propositional calculus.

doubt, method of

the starting-point for Descartes's philosophy. He used perceptual illusions, the dream problem and the possibility of a deceiving God, to show the uncertainty of many common beliefs. Only the cogito then survives as an indubitable foundation for knowledge.

doxa (dóxa)

Greek term for opinion, belief or judgement, as opposed to systematic knowledge (Gk. episthmh [epistêmê]). According to Plato, this limited awareness of the sensible world encompasses the lower portion of the divided line. In Aristotle's works on logic, the same terms are used to distinguish contingent from necessary truths about the world.

dualism, mind-body

belief that mental things and physical things are fundamentally distinct kinds of entities. As a solution to the traditional mind-body problem, dualism derives especially from Descartes and his followers in the seventeenth century. Variations on this theme (including interactionism, parallelism and epiphenomenalism) arise when dualists try to explain why events in the supposedly separate realms of mind and body seem so well coordinated with each other.

Du Bois, William Edward Burghardt (1868-1963)

American historian and sociologist. After completing his education with a Ph.D. from Harvard, Du Bois embarked on a long and distinguished career as a university professor and social activist. His The Souls of Black Folk (1903) was a penetrating analysis of the origins, practices and consequences of racial discrimination in the United States. Du Bois also participated in efforts at social reform, founding the National Association fot the Advancement of Colored People in 1910 and editing the influential journals Crisis and Phylon. Details of Du Bois's life are to be found in his autobiography, Dusk of Dawn (1940).

Duhem, Pierre M. M. (1861-1916)

French historian and philosopher of science. In La Théorie physique: son objet et sa structure (The Aim and Structure of Physical Theory) (1906), Duhem maintained that every scientific theory is an exercise in metaphysical speculation, verified or falsified by the predictive power it is shown to have as a systematic whole.

Dummett, Michael A. E. (1925-)

English philosopher and logician. The essays collected in Truth and other Enigmas (1978) and The Seas of Language (1993) defend an intuitionist philosophy of mathematics and emphasise the linguistic foundations of epistemology. Dummett is also the foremost English interpreter of Frege in such works as Frege: Philosophy of Language (1973), The Interpretation of Frege's Philosophy (1981) and Frege: Philosophy of Mathematics (1991).

dunamiV (dynamis)

Greek term for power or force, used by pre-socratic philosophers in reference to the qualities or features of material elements. Aristotle later used the term to signify potentiality or the capacity for undergoing change. The neoplatonic tradition, on the other hand, developed a conception of personified causal agents.

Durkheim, Émile (1858-1917)

French philosopher and sociologist. Durkheim argued that since society is something more than merely a collection of individual human beings, it follows that social events cannot be explained wholly in biological or psychological terms. This insight was a significant impetus for the independence of sociology as a science. His major writings include Éléments de sociologie (1889), Les Règles de la méthode sociologique (Rules for Sociological Method) (1895), De la division du travail social (The Division of Labor in Society)

(1893) and Le Suicide (Suicide: A Study in Sociology) (1897). Durkheim criticised pragmatism in Pragmatism and Society (1914).

■ **duties**

what we ought to do. An action that people are required to perform, it is the practical content of a moral obligation.

■ **Dworkin, Ronald Myles (1931-)**

American political philosopher. In Taking Rights Seriously (1977) and Law's Empire (1986), Dworkin defends a version of legal positivism that relies heavily upon the principled adjudication of disputes by the judiciary. His treatment of concrete legal issues concerning abortion and euthanasia is to be found in Life's Dominion (1993). 'Objectivity and Truth: You'd Better Believe It' argues that a moderate notion of objectivity secures the objectivity of moral claims.

■ **'E' proposition**

in the traditional notation for categorical logic, a proposition that is both universal and negative. Example: 'No reptiles are insects.' This proposition affirms that no individual is both a reptile and an insect. Its contradictory is an 'I' proposition with the same subject and predicate terms.

■ **ecofeminism**

belief that human violation of the natural world is an extension of the prevalent patriarchy of Western culture. On this view, efforts to protect the environment at large are feminist in spirit, since they challenge systemic male domination of the other.

■ **effect (Ger. Wirkung)**

an event that is taken to result from or to be produced by another event, with which it stands in a causal relationship.

■ **efficient cause**

the agent or event that produces some change in the accidental features of a thing. One of Aristotle's four causes.

■ **egoism**

belief that human conduct is governed by self-interest. Psychological egoism holds that all human beings are, as a matter of fact, motivated to act only in pursuit of their own (at least apparent) advantage, never for the sake of others. Ethical egoism is the normative theory that right conduct can be defined in terms of (an enlightened notion of) one's own welfare. Though often held jointly, the distinction between fact and value clearly renders the two views distinct: some might argue that human beings ought to act on their own behalf, even though they don't always do so, while others could suppose that they invariably do act selfishly even though they ought not.

■ eidos (eidos)

Greek term for what is seen, figure, shape or form. In the philosophy of Plato, the eidos is the immutable genuine nature of a thing, one of the eternal, transcendent Forms apprehended by human reason (Gk. nouV [nous]). Aristotle rejected the notion of independently existing Forms and understood them instead as abstract universals. By extension, Husserl used the term 'eidetic' for the phenomenological apprehension of essences generally.

■ eikasia (eikásia)

Greek term used by Plato, to signify human imagination, which is focussed exclusively on a temporal appearance or image (Gk. eikwn).

■ Eleatics

pre-socratic philosophers, including Parmenides and Zeno, who used dialectical methods to argue that reality is a unified whole, within which no motion or change is possible.

■ eliminativism

belief that language should be purged of all reference to the (non-existent) things of a certain kind. It is the most extreme variety of reductionism. Thus, while a reductive materialist may hold that pains are really just activities of the central nervous system, an eliminative materialist proposes that we speak only of brain-states.

■ emanation

that which inevitably flows outward from the transcendental central principle of reality ('the One') in the neoplatonic philosophy of Plotinus. Individual things, including human beings, are therefore presumed to be nothing more than the faint ripples left by a primordial big splash. The timeless reality of a central intelligence, Plotinus held, inexorably results in the formation of both, soul as an active principle of organisation and, eventually, inert matter.

■ emergent property

an irreducible feature (now commonly called supervenient) of a complex whole that cannot be inferred directly from the features of its simpler parts. Thus, for example, the familiar taste of salt is an emergent property, with respect to the sodium and chlorine of which it is composed.

■ emotion, appeal to (argumentum ad populum)

the informal fallacy of persuading someone to accept (or reject) a conclusion by arousing favourable (or unfavourable) emotions towards it or by emphasising its widespread acceptance (or rejection) by others. Example: 'Nobody with an ounce of common sense or a single shred of integrity believes that our President is truly an effective leader. Therefore, the President is not an effective leader.'

■ emotive meaning

attitudes and feelings associated with the use of a word, phrase or sentence, in contrast with its literal significance.

■ emotivism

the meta-ethical theory according to which the meaning of moral language is exhausted by its expression, evocation or endorsement of powerful human feelings. Thus, for example, saying 'Stealing is wrong', is just an especially strong way of reporting that I disapprove of stealing, evoking a similar disapproval from others and thereby attempting to influence future conduct, both mine and theirs. Although its origins lie in the non-cognitivist morality of Hume, emotivism reached its height early in the twentieth century, with the work of the logical positivists and Stevenson.

■ empirical (Ger. Erfahrung)
based on use of the senses, observation or experience, generally. Hence, the empirical coincides with what is a posteriori.

■ empiricism
reliance on experience as the source of ideas and knowledge. More specifically, empiricism is the epistemological theory that genuine information about the world must be acquired by a posteriori means, so that nothing can be thought without first being sensed. Prominent modern empiricists include Bacon, Locke, Berkeley, Hume and Mill. In the twentieth century, empiric principles were extended and applied by the pragmatists and the logical positivists.

■ encyclopedists
a group of French philosophers, including Condillac, d'Alembert, d'Holbach, Diderot, Helvetius, Montesquieu, Rousseau, Turgot and Voltaire, who expressed their anti-institutional views on morality, politics and religion in the seventeen-volume Encyclopédie ou dictionnaire raisonné des sciences, des arts, et des métiers (Encyclopedia, or a Descriptive Dictionary of the Sciences, Arts, and Trades) (1751-1772), a generative text of the French Enlightenment.

■ end (Gk. teloV [télos])
the goal or purpose of a thing. Hence, in the philosophy of Aristotle, the final cause.

■ energeia (energeia)
Greek term for the operation or activity of anything. More technically, in the philosophy of Aristotle, energeia is the actuality characteristic of every individual substance towards some end, in contrast with its potentiality or capacity to change.

■ enlightenment (Ger. Auflkärung)
an eighteenth-century movement that placed great emphasis on the use of reason in the development of philo-

sophical, social, political and scientific knowledge. Enlightenment philosophers include Bayle, Hume, Wollstonecraft, Kant and many lesser figures.

■ entailment

relation between propositions, such that one of them is strictly implied by the other(s). That is, its falsity is logically impossible, given the truth of what entails it. Thus, the premises of a valid deductive argument entail its conclusion.

■ entäusserung and entfremdung

German terms used by Hegel and Marx for alienation or estrangement from one's own nature.

■ enteleceia (entelecheia)

Aristotle's Greek term for the complete reality or perfection of a thing, as the soul is of the human body. For Leibniz an 'entelechy' is the active force resident in every monad.

■ enthusiasm

an exaggerated state of religious fervour or reliance on divine inspiration. Enlightenment philosophers such as Locke and Leibniz decried manifestations of enthusiasm as incompatible with the proper employment of rational faculties.

■ enthymeme

a deductive argument (especially a categorical syllogism) from whose ordinary-language expression one or more propositions have been omitted or left unstated.

■ Epictetus (55-135)

Stoic philosopher whose Manual set forth the conditions under which one may live well (even as a slave) by distinguishing correctly between things under our control (our desires and feelings) and things not under our control (events and circumstances).

■ Epicurus (341-270 BCE)

Greek philosopher who explored the moral consequences of ancient atomism.

■ epiphenomenalism
belief that consciousness is an incidental side-effect ('epiphenomenon') or by-product of physical or mechanical reality. On this view, although mental events are in some sense real, they have no causal efficacy in the material realm.

■ episthmh (epistêmê)
Greek term for an organised body of theoretical knowledge. According to Plato, this encompasses the upper portion of the divided line. In the philosophy of Aristotle, episthmh is a body of demonstrable truths about the essences of things.

■ epistemology
branch of philosophy that investigates the possibility, origins, nature and extent of human knowledge. Although the effort to develop an adequate theory of knowledge is at least as old as Plato's Theaetetus, epistemology has dominated Western philosophy only since the era of Descartes and Locke, as an extended dispute between rationalism and empiricism over the respective importance of a priori and a posteriori origins. Contemporary postmodern thinkers (including many feminist philosophers) have proposed the contextualisation of knowledge as part of an intersubjective process.

■ epoch (epochê)
Greek term for cessation or stoppage. Hence, in the philosophy of the sceptics, the suspension of judgement. Only by refusing either to affirm or to deny the truth of what we cannot know, they supposed, can we achieve the ataraxia [ataraxia] of a peaceful mind.

■ equivalence
relation between two propositions, either of which may be inferred from the other.

p	q	p°q
T	T	T
T	F	F
F	T	F
F	F	T

A material equivalence, symbolised here in the form: p ° q, is a compound statement that is true whenever both of its component statements have the same truth-value.

■ equivocal
having more than one meaning.

■ equivocation
the informal fallacy that can result when an ambiguous word or phrase is used in different senses, within a single argument. Example: 'Odd things arouse human suspicion. But seventeen is an odd number. Therefore, seventeen arouses human suspicion.'

■ Erfahrung
German term for empirical observation.

■ Erlebnis
German term for experience generally.

■ eroV (eros)
Greek personification of love. Hence, sexual desire or love generally. Plato's Symposium offers a set of speeches on the nature of love in human life.

■ esse est percipi
Latin phrase meaning 'to be is to be perceived'. According to Berkeley, this is the most basic feature of all sensible objects. For spirits, on the other hand, esse est percipere ('to be is to perceive'). Granting this to be the most fundamental principle of idealistic philosophy, Moore argued that it is indefensible.

■ essence / accident (Lat. per se / per accidens)
distinction among the attributes, properties or qualities of substances. A thing's possession of its essential properties is necessary either for its individual existence or, at least, for its membership in a specific kind. Accidental features, by contrast, are those which the thing merely happens to have, even though it need not. Thus, for example, rationality may be part of the essence of any human being, but being able to calculate square roots accurately in one's head is (surely) an accident.

■ estrangement
withdrawal from things or people.

■ eternal return
belief that everything that happens has happened before

and will happen again, since the universe (or time itself) is fundamentally cyclical. A standard feature of Pythagorean and Stoic thought, this view was more recently adopted as a basis for practical hope by Nietzsche.

■ ethics

branch of philosophy concerned with the evaluation of human conduct. Philosophers commonly distinguish:

Descriptive ethics, the factual study of the ethical standards or principles of a group or tradition.

Normative ethics, the development of theories that systematically denominate right and wrong actions.

Applied ethics, the use of these theories to form judgements regarding practical cases.

Meta-ethics, careful analysis of the meaning and justification of ethical claims.

■ eqos (ethos)

Greek word for custom or habit, the characteristic conduct of an individual human life. Hence, beginning with Aristotle, ethics is the study of human conduct and the Stoics held that all behaviour, for good or evil, arises from the eqos of the individual.

■ eudaemonism

an approach to ethics (as proposed, for example, by Aristotle or the Stoics) that aims at the achievement of a good life. Classical eudaemonism is concerned with satisfying the objective conditions of happiness, rather than with pursuing the subjective experience of pleasure. Kant condemned this approach to human conduct as heteronomous.

■ evidence

support for the truth of a proposition, especially that

derived from empirical observation or experience.

■ evil, problem of

bad things sometimes happen. Whether they are taken to flow from the operation of the world ('natural evil'), to result from deliberate human cruelty ('moral evil') or simply to correlate poorly with what seems to be deserved ('non-karmic evil'), such events give rise to basic questions about whether or not life is fair.

■ excluded middle, principle of

logical principle that propositions of the form (p Ú ~ p) are tautologous. Thus, for example:
'Either it will snow today or it will not snow today.' is necessarily true.
Note the difference between excluded middle and bivalence.

■ exclusive premises

the formal fallacy committed in a categorical syllogism that is invalid because both of its premises are negative.
Example: 'Since no mammals are fish and some fish are not whales, it follows that some whales are not mammals.'

■ existence

instantiation in reality or actual being. Kant pointed out that existence is not a predicate, and Frege proposed that it is a second-order property of those first-order properties that happen to be instantiated. The metaphysical question of what kinds of things exist is the subject of ontology, as is the even more general question of why there is something rather than nothing.

■ existential fallacy

the formal fallacy committed in a categorical syllogism that is invalid because it has two universal premises and a particular conclusion.
Example: 'All inhabitants of another planet are friendly people and all Martians are inhabitants of another planet. Therefore, some Martians are friendly people.'

■ existential generalisation

a quantification rule of the form:
Øu.

($x)(Øx).
Example: 'Polly is a bird. Therefore, there is at least one bird.'
This pattern of reasoning is one of the basic principles used by proofs in quantification theory.

■ **existential import**
the distinguishing feature of propositions that assert the existence of something. In traditional interpretations of categorical logic, all propositions are taken to have existential import, but on a modern interpretation, only the particular propositions, (I and O) have existential import.

■ **existential instantiation**
a quantification rule of the form:
($x)(Øx).
Øu.
Example: 'There is at least one bird. Therefore, suppose that some particular thing, z, is a bird.'
Properly applied, this pattern of reasoning provides an important basis for proofs in quantification theory.

■ **existentialism**
a (mostly) twentieth-century approach that emphasises the primacy of individual existence over any presumed natural essence for human beings. Although they differ on many details, existentialists generally suppose that the fact of my existence as a human being entails both my unqualified freedom to make of myself whatever I will and the awesome responsibility of employing that freedom appropriately, without being driven by anxiety towards escaping into the inauthenticity or self-deception of any conventional set of rules for behaviour, even though the entire project may turn out to be absurd.

■ **expected value**
the net return, it is reasonable to anticipate as the result of an action or investment. Expected value may be calculated as the sum of the products of each possible outcome and the relative likelihood that it will occur.

■ explanation

an intelligible account of why something happens. On a covering law model, the scientific explanation of an event has the form of an argument whose conclusion is the event to be explained and whose premises include both antecedent circumstances and one or more hypothesis.

■ exportation (exp.)

a rule of replacement of the form:

[(p ·q) É r)] º [p É (q É r)]

Example: 'If Harry is tall and quick, then he plays well.' is equivalent to 'If Harry is tall, then if he's quick, then he plays well.'

The reliability of this equivalence is evident from a truth-table.

■ extrinsic

bearing some relation to something else.

■ fact / value

distinction between assertions about how things really are (fact) and how things ought to be (value). Drawn by Hume, but also defended by Stevenson, Hare and other ethical noncognitivists, the distinction is usually taken to entail that claims about moral obligation can never be validly inferred from the truth of factual premises alone. It follows that people who agree completely on the simple description of a state of affairs may nevertheless differ with respect to the appropriate action to take in response to it.

■ facticity

the contingent conditions of an individual human life. In the existentialism of Heidegger and Sartre, facticity includes all of the concrete details, time and place of birth, for example, along with the prospect of death, against the background of which human freedom is to be exercised.

■ fallacy

a mistake in reasoning. An argument that fails to provide adequate logical support for the truth of its conclusion, yet appears convincing or persuasive in some other way. Common examples include both formal fallacies (structural errors in deductive logic) and informal fallacies (efforts to persuade by non-rational appeals).

■ **fallibilism**

belief that some or all claims to knowledge could be mistaken. Although Peirce limited the application of fallibilism to the empirical statements of natural science, Quine extended it by challenging the notion that any proposition can be genuinely analytic. Unlike a sceptic, the fallibilist may not demand suspension of belief in the absence of certainty.

■ **false cause**

the informal fallacy of affirming the presence of a causal relationship on anything less than adequate grounds. Post hoc, ergo propter hoc is a common variety of this fallacy.

Example: 'After drinking milk for twenty years, Melanie became addicted to cocaine. Therefore, drinking milk caused her cocaine addiction.'

■ **falsifiability**

a property of any proposition for which it is possible to specify a set of circumstances, the occurrence of which would demonstrate that the proposition is false. According to Karl Popper, falsifiability is the crucial feature of scientific hypothesis: beliefs that can never be tested against the empirical evidence are dogmatic.

■ **fatalism**

belief that every event is bound to happen, as it does not matter what we do about it. Fatalism is the most extreme form of causal determinism, since it denies that human actions have any causal efficacy. Any determinist holds that indigestion is the direct consequence of natural causes, but the fatalist believes that it is bound to occur whether or not I eat spicy foods.

■ **feminism**

commitment to the abolition of male domination in human society. Feminists differ widely in their accounts of the origins of patriarchy, their analysis of its most common consequences and their concrete proposals for overcoming it, but all share in the recognition that the subordination of women to men in our culture is indefensible and eliminable. Many feminist philosophers oppose Cartesian dualism, scientific objectivity and traditional theories of moral obligation, as instances of masculine over-reliance on reason.

■ Ferio

name given by mediaeval logicians to any categorical syllogism whose standard form may be designated as EIO-1. Example: No mendicant friars are wealthy patrons of the arts, but some mediaeval philosophers are mendicant friars, so some mediaeval philosophers are not wealthy patrons of the arts.

■ Ferison

name given by mediaeval logicians to any categorical syllogism whose standard form is EIO-3. Example: Since no people who admire Marx are political conservatives and some people who admire Marx are South Carolinians, it follows that some South Carolinians are not political conservatives.

■ Festino

name given by mediaeval logicians to a categorical syllogism with the standard form EIO-2. Example: No people deserving of our admiration and praise are inveterate liars, but some wealthy industrialists are inveterate liars. Therefore, some wealthy industrialists are not people deserving of our admiration and praise.

■ Fibonacci Leonardo Pisano (1170-1250)

Italian mathematician. After travelling in North Africa, Fibonacci wrote Liber Abaci (1202), introducing the use of Arabic numerals for the decimal system into European arithmetic. His Liber quadratorum

(Book of Square Numbers) (1225) introduced the 'Fibonacci series' of natural numbers: 0, 1, 1, 2, 3 ,5 ,8, 13, ..., each element of which is the sum of the preceding two.

■ **Ficino, Marsillio (1433-1499)**

Italian philosopher whose translations into Latin made the works of Plato and Plotinus accessible during the Renaissance. Despite his fascination with myth and magic, Ficino endorsed a synthesis of neo-platonic thought with the doctrines of Christianity.

■ **fideism**

belief that religious doctrines rest exclusively on faith (Lat. Fides), instead of on reason. In various forms, fideism was maintained by philosophers as diverse as Pascal, Bayle and Kierkegaard.

■ **figure**

a systematic way of indicating the position of the middle term in a categorical syllogism.

■ **five ways**

the attempts to prove the existence of God, included in Thomas Aquinas's Summa Theologica 1, 2, 3. They include three versions of the cosmological argument, an argument from moral perfection and the teleological argument.

■ **force, appeal to (argumentum ad baculum)**

the informal fallacy of securing agreement by threatening adverse consequences in case of disagreement. Example: 'Anyone who believes that the government has exceeded its proper authority under the constitution will be subjected to severe harassment by the provincial police. Therefore, the government has not exceeded its authority.'

■ **formal cause**

structural features or attributes of a thing, one of the four causes.

■ **forms, platonic (Gk. eide [eide])**

the pure objects of mathematical and dialectical knowledge. In the vigorous realism of Plato's middle dialogues, necessary truths are taken to involve knowledge of eternal, unchanging Forms (or Ideas). Particular things in the realm of appearance are beautiful, or equal, or good, only insofar as they participate in the universal Forms of Beauty, Equality, or the Good. The doctrine of Forms was attacked in Plato's own Parmenides and by Aristotle.

■ four terms, fallacy of (quaternio terminorum)

the formal fallacy committed in a categorical syllogism that is invalid because it employs more than three distinct categorical terms. Example: 'All managers are politicians and all sybarites are administrators, so all sybarites are politicians.'

■ freedom (Lat. libertas Ger. Freiheit)

the human capacity to act (or not to act) as we choose or prefer, without any external compulsion or restraint. Freedom in this sense is usually regarded as a presupposition of moral responsibility: the actions for which I may be praised or blamed, rewarded or punished, are just those which I perform freely.

■ Fresison

name given by mediaeval logicians to any categorical syllogism whose standard form may be designated as EIO-4. Example: Since no fish are mammals while some animals that live in water are mammals, it follows that some animals that live in water are not fish.

■ functionalism

an approach to the philosophy of mind that analyses mental states in terms of what they do, rather than of what they are. This focus on activities performed instead of on intrinsic features, often taken to parallel the difference between software and hardware in a Turing machine, may help to avoid many thorny problems.

■ fuzzy logic

non-classical system of reasoning, in which propositions may have many degrees of truth or falsity. Developed by Lofti Zadeh as a method of providing for vagueness in the application of predicates, fuzzy logic has found a number of significant practical applications in the design and operation of control-systems.

■ Gadamer, Hans-Georg (1900-2002)

German philosopher. A student of Nicolai Hartmann. In Wahrheit und Methode, Grundzüge einer philosophischen Hermaneutik (Truth and Method) (1960), Philosophical Hermeneutics (1977), Reason in the Age of Science (1983), Gadamer develops a hermeneutic according to which the meaning of any text is a function of the historical situations of both author and interpreter. Since each reading is grounded in its own context, no one reading offers a definitive or final interpretation of the text. The virtual dialogue continues indefinitely.

■ Gandhi, Mohandas Karamchand (1869-1948)

Indian political leader, also called 'Mahatma' (the Great-Souled). In opposition to racial discrimination against Indian nationals in South Africa and to British colonial rule of India itself, Gandhi urged the practice of Satyagraha, in a practical effort to achieve peaceful resolution of political differences as head of the Indian National Congress. *Constructive Programme: Its Meaning and Place* (1941) includes a detailed description of the method he espoused. Active in efforts to reduce Hindu-Muslim ethnic conflict, Gandhi himself was assassinated by a Hindu fanatic.

■ Gauss, Carl Friedrich (1777-1855).

German physicist and mathematician. Gauss established the foundations of modern number theory with his work on primes in *Disquisitiones arithmeticae* (1801) and contributed significantly to the study of electromagnetic forces. Gauss was the teacher of Riemann and Dedekind.

■ Gemeinschaft / Gesellschaft

German distinction between community, characterised by

traditional practices and a personal sense of belonging, and the more individualistic, competitive and impersonal organisation of mere society.

■ gender/sex

distinction between the socially-constructed expectations associated with masculinity and femininity and the biological categories of male and female. De Beauvoir, MacKinnon and other feminists drew attention to the disparate power relationships established by gender differentiation in our culture.

■ general will (Fr. volonté générale)

collective desire for the welfare of a society as a whole. According to Jean Jacques Rousseau, the citizens of a properly contracted civil society are infallibly guided by the general will, rather than by their conflicting individual self-interests.

■ genus and differentia

Latin terms used by mediaeval logicians, in an effort to define a term by indicating the general kind (genus) of things to which it refers and then specifying the special feature (differentia) which sets them apart from other things of the same kind. This usage derives from Aristotle's logic, where the highest kind to which an individual thing belongs is one of the basic categories of being.

■ Gettier, Edmund (1927-)

American philosopher, whose Is Justified True Belief Knowledge? (1963), offers counter-examples to show that even justified true belief may not be genuine knowledge in cases where that which justifies one's belief happens not to be related directly to the truth of what one believes.

■ Glück

German term for happiness.

■ gnwsiV (gnôsis)

the most general Greek term for knowledge. Thus, Aristotle took it to include both accurate understanding and sensory experience of the natural world. From the second century CE onward, the

'Gnostics' used the term to signify the theological secrets they supposed crucial for genuine Christianity.

■ God, existence of

attempts to demonstrate the existence of God have been a notable feature of Western philosophy. The most commonly employed theistic efforts include: the cosmological argument, the ontological argument, the teleological argument and the moral argument. The most serious atheological argument is the problem of evil.

■ good

the most general term of approval, both moral and non-moral, whether intrinsic or extrinsic.

■ greatest happiness principle

the definition of moral value by utilitarians. As stated by Hutcheson, Bentham, and Mill, the principle is that actions are right, only insofar as they tend to produce the greatest balance of pleasure over pain for the largest number of people.

■ Grosseteste, Robert (1170-1253)

English philosopher. Grosseteste used Arabic and Jewish commentaries on the philosophy of Aristotle to develop his own scientific and religious theories, using practical experimentation to study the nature of light.

■ grue

a colour-predicate used by Goodman to illustrate a significant problem with inductive predictions. With respect to a designated future time, an object is grue if it is seen to be green when first observed before that time or if it is seen to be blue when first observed after that time. The problem is that our present observations of green grass seem to provide equal support for hypothesis that grass is green and that grass is grue (or gred, for that matter). There is no simple and apparent way of forestalling this gruesome difficulty.

■ haecceity (Lat. haecceitas)

thisness, the property that uniquely distinguishes each

individual thing from others of its kind. Introduced by Duns Scotus as a name for the individuating essence of any particular, the term has been used more recently in connection with the view that rigidly designated individuals can exist in each of many possible worlds.

Hamilton, William (1788-1856)

Scottish philosopher, author of Lectures on Metaphysics and Logic (1860). Hamilton followed Reid in defending common sense against the scepticism of empiricists like Hume Hamilton's thought was subjected, in turn, to sharp criticism by Mill.

happiness (Gk. eudaimonia [eudaimonia], Ger. Glück)

general well-being in human life, an important goal for many people and a significant issue for theories in normative ethics. Aristotle disagreed with the identification of happiness with bodily pleasure, defended by Aristippus and other hedonists. Most utilitarians accept this identification, but emphasise the importance of considering the greatest happiness of everyone rather than merely one's own.

Haraway, Donna Jeanne (1944-)

American feminist philosopher of science who proposes a fundamental re-examination of the concepts of human nature and political identity in light of post-modern rejection of stark dualisms. Her 'Manifesto for Cyborgs' (1965) suggests that the extent of our reliance on technology makes it difficult to understand ourselves independently of mechanical devices. Although we are all fabricated hybrids of organism and machine, Haraway supposes that feminist cyborgs have the opportunity to escape the perils of patriarchal capitalist technology.

Harding, Sandra (1935-)

American philosopher of science. In Discovering Reality: Feminist Perspectives on Epistemology, Methodology and Philosophy of Science (with

Merrill Hintikka) (1983), The Science Question in Feminism (1986) and Whose Science? Whose Knowledge?: Thinking from Women's Lives (1991), Harding shows that it may be possible to eliminate such basic concepts of traditional Western epistemology as 'objectivity', 'universality' and 'duality'. Doing so would create the possibility of alternative ways of thinking, grounded in fundamentally different standpoints, including a feminist perspective borne of women's experience of reality.

hedonism

belief that pleasure (Gk. 'hdonh [hêdonê]) is the highest or only source of intrinsic value. Although commonly defended as a moral theory about the proper aim of human conduct, hedonism is usually grounded on the psychological claim that human beings simply do act in such ways as to maximise their own happiness. Aristotle argued against any attempt to identify pleasure as the highest good, but Epicurus held that physical pleasure and freedom from pain are significant goals for human life. The utilitarianism of Bentham proposes a practical method for calculating hedonic value.

Hegel, Georg W.F. (1770-1831)

German philosopher who employed a dialectical logic (moving from thesis to antithesis to synthesis) and its corollary analysis of historical inevitability, in support of an idealism in which human culture is properly seen as a manifestation of the self-consciousness of the Absolute.

Heidegger, Martin (1889-1976)

German philosopher who used the techniques of Husserl's phenomenology in a more openly metaphysical programme, which resulted in the development of existentialism.

■ hermeneutics
formal study of appropriate methods of interpretation, first developed as a formal discipline of study by Schleiermacher. Following the work of Dilthey, Gadamer and Ricouer, the hermeneutical process is often regarded as involving a complex interaction between the interpreting subject and the interpreted object. The task is complicated by the apparent circularity of understanding particular elements in light of the text as a whole, which can in turn be understood only by reference to them.

■ heteronomy
submission to the moral authority of external influences, hope or fear.

■ heterological
self-referentially inapplicable.

■ heuristic
an informal method for solving problems in the absence of an algorithm for formal proof. Heuristics typically have only restricted applicability and limited likelihood of success but, as George Polya showed, contribute significantly to our understanding of mathematical truths.

■ historicism
belief that social structures, events and texts are best to be understood in the context of their historical development. Versions of this view were defended by Dilthey, Lukacs, and Gramsci. More recently, Popper and Hayek criticised the extreme version of this view, according to which the historical outcomes are inevi-

tably determined. In the milder form embraced by Croce, Kuhn and Gadamer, however, historicism is simply the notion that a purely ahistorical perspective on human affairs would be misleading.

■ Hobbes, Thomas (1588-1679)

British philosopher who used the principles of a materialist physics to defend ethical egoism and a social contract theory of the state.

■ homological / heterological

distinction between concepts or words. A homological term applies to itself, a heterological term does not. Thus, for example: 'short' and 'having fewer than ten syllables' are homological terms; 'big' and 'having more than ten syllables' are heterological terms.

■ homonymous / synonymous / paronymous

Aristotle's distinction among different uses of a term: they are said to be homonymous if the uses are entirely distinct, synonymous if they are the same and paronymous if they are different but related. Thus, for example:

In 'Colleen is a cat' and 'Garfield is a cat' 'cat' is used homonymously.

In 'Carter was president in 1978' and 'Bush was president in 1990' 'president' is used synonymously.

In 'Jean was brave' and 'What Jean did was brave' 'brave' is used paronymously.

■ humanism

belief that individual human beings are the fundamental source of all value and have the ability to understand and perhaps even to control the natural world by careful application of their own rational faculties. During the Renaissance, humanists such as Bruno, Erasmus, Valla and Pico della Mirandola helped shift attention away from arcane theological disputes towards more productive avenues of classical study and natural science.

■ **hylomorphic**

Aristotle's theory that natural objects are irreducible composites of matter and form.

■ **hypostasisation**

the variety of reification that results from supposing that whatever can be named or conceived abstractly must actually exist. When (in Through the Looking Glass) his Messenger declares "I'm sure nobody walks much faster than I do," the White King hypostasises 'Nobody', by responding that "He can't do that or else he'd have been here first." Such philosophers as Plato, Hegel and Heidegger are sometimes accused of similar flights of ontological whimsy.

■ **hypothesis**

a general principle, tentatively put forward for the purposes of scientific explanation and subject to disconfirmation by empirical evidence.

■ **hypothetical imperative**

a conditional moral demand.

■ **idea (Ger. Begriff)**

the content of conscious thought. Plato used the Greek word 'idea' to designate the universal Forms. For modern representationalists like Descartes and Locke, however, ideas are the immediate objects of every mental activity. Ideas in this sense are supposed to represent things, present or absent, before the mind.

■ **idealism**

belief that only mental entities are real, so that physical things exist only in the sense that they are perceived. Berkeley defended his 'immaterialism' on purely empiricist grounds, while Kant and Fichte arrived at theirs by transcendental arguments. German, English and (to a lesser degree) American philosophy during the nineteenth century was dominated by the monistic absolute idealism of Hegel, Bradley and Royce.

identity

the logical relation of numerical sameness, in which each thing stands only to itself. Although everything is what it is and not anything else, philosophers try to formulate more precisely the criteria by means of which we may be sure that one and the same thing is cognised under two different descriptions or at two distinct times. Leibniz held that numerical identity is equivalent to indiscernibility or sameness of all the features each thing has. But Locke maintained that judgements of identity are invariably made by reference to types or sorts of things. The identity of individual persons is an especially troublesome case.

identity theory of mind

belief that mental properties and events are identical with physical properties and events. Although the details are not yet apparent, identity theorists suppose that scientific research into the nature of the central nervous system will eventually establish the contingent identity of every kind of conscious experience with some neurophysiological phenomenon. Significant variations of the identity theory include physicalism and neutral monism.

ignorance, appeal to (argumentum ad ignoratiam)

the informal fallacy of supposing that a proposition must be true because there is no proof that it is false. Example: 'The F.B.I. investigation was never able to establish that Smith was not at the scene of the crime on the night of June 25, so we may safely conclude that he was there.'

ignoratio elenchi

Latin phrase meaning, 'misunderstanding of the refutation'.

illicit major

the formal fallacy committed in a categorical syllogism that is invalid because its major term is undistributed in the major premise but distributed in the conclusion. Example: 'All dogs are mammals. No cats are dogs. Therefore, no cats are mammals.'

illicit minor
the formal fallacy committed in a categorical syllogism that is invalid because its minor term is undistributed in the minor premise but distributed in the conclusion. Example: 'All poodles are mammals. All poodles are pets. Therefore, All pets are mammals.'

illocutionary act
the speech act of doing something else, offering advice or taking a vow, for example, in the process of uttering meaningful language. Thus, for example, in saying 'I will repay you this money next week', one typically performs the illocutionary act of making a promise.

imagination (Gk. eikasia [eikásia])
the capacity to consider sensible objects without actually perceiving them or supposing that they really exist. Philosophers have disagreed over whether or not acts of imagination necessarily involve mental images or ideas.

immediate inference
the relationship between two propositions that are logically equivalent. In categorical logic, the traditional immediate inferences include: conversion, obversion and contraposition.

impartiality
the absence of any bias towards or away from a particular person or opinion. Enlightenment philosophers often upheld the use of human reason as an impartial tool, but post-modern thinkers raise significant doubts about the possibility and value of such objectivity. Although moral impartiality has traditionally been regarded as a virtue, in strict practice, it would require callous disregard for every special relationship with another person. In public life, however, impartiality is a crucial component of justice.

incommensurability
incapable of being measured against a common standard. The presumed incommensurability of individual human pleasures is sometimes raised as an objection against hedonistic versions of utilitarianism. Feyerabend and Kuhn

suppose that rival scientific theories are incommensurable if neither can be fully stated in the vocabulary of the other.

■ incontinence

inability to act reasonably because of weakness of will, lack of self-control.

■ incorrigible

incapable of being corrected, hence, a putative criterion of certainty. An incorrigible proposition is one about which it is impossible to be mistaken, such as (perhaps) 'I am now in pain.' Whether any human knowledge is actually incorrigible is one of the central questions of epistemology.

■ indexical

an expression whose meaning depends upon the context in which it is employed. Thus, for example, in the sentence, 'I came back from there an hour ago', the words 'I' and 'there', along with the phrase 'an hour ago', are all indexicals, the person, place and time to which they refer is different on each occasion of their use.

■ indirect proof

demonstration of the truth of a proposition from the impossible consequences of its contradictory.

■ individual constant

a symbol (usually lowercase letters such as a, b, c, etc.) used to represent a specific thing in quantification theory.

■ individual variable

a symbol (usually lowercase letters such as x, y, z, etc.) used to represent any individual generally in quantification theory.

■ indubitable

the characteristic of a proposition whose truth cannot be doubted, such as 'My father is older than I am', even though (given bizarre suppositions about time and/or human conception) it might be false. Descartes and other modern philosophers supposed that only such propositions would provide a suitable foundation for human knowledge.

induction
probable reasoning whose conclusion goes beyond what is formally contained in its premises.

ineffable
incapable of being expressed in language, as the experience of qualia generally and mystical insight, in particular, are sometimes held to be.

inference
the relationship that holds between the premises and the conclusion of a logical argument or the process of drawing a conclusion from premises that support it deductively or inductively.

infinite regress
a definitional, explanatory or justificatory procedure that entails its own reapplication without any limit. Thus, for example, the claim that everything in the world has only extrinsic value, would lead to an infinite regress. Since the lack of any intrinsically worthwhile starting-point would render all value open to question, the procedure seems to be self-defeating.

informative use of language
communication employed for the purpose of asserting propositions or presenting arguments.

ingenium
Latin term for natural capacity or understanding.

innate ideas
mental contents that are presumed to exist in the mind prior to and independently of any experience.

instrumentalism
belief that statements or theories may be used as tools for useful prediction, without reference to their possible truth or falsity. Peirce and other pragmatists defended an instrumentalist account of modern science.

intention
the meaning of an expression.

intentionality
the characteristic feature of cognitive states, that they invariably represent or are about something beyond themselves. The intentions of a moral agent are, therefore, the states of mind that accompany its actions.

■ **interactionism**
the supposition, defended by Descartes and others, that the minds and bodies of human beings exert direct causal influence on each other, even though they are distinct substances of different kinds.

■ **intertextuality**
the complex mosaic of relationships by means of which signifiers have meaning in the semantic theories of Lyotard and Kristeva.

■ **intrinsic / extrinsic**
distinction between the features of things. The intrinsic features of a thing are those which it has in and of itself, while its extrinsic features are those which it has only in its relation to something else. Thus, for example, I am intrinsically a human being, but only extrinsically a father. It might reasonably be disputed whether my being male is an intrinsic biological feature or an extrinsic cultural construction.

■ **intuition (Gk. nohsiV [nóêsis])**
direct, non-inferential awareness of abstract objects or concrete truths. Plato held that intuition is a superior faculty and Spinoza supposed that intuition is the highest sort of human knowledge. Russell, on the other hand, designated as intuitive any unreflective instance of knowledge by acquaintance.

■ **intuitionism**
reliance on unmediated awareness as a criterion of truth. In logic and mathematics, intuitionism denies the independent reality of mathematical objects and the principle of excluded middle. In moral philosophy, intuitionism is the metaethical theory that moral judgements are made by reference to a direct, non-inferential awareness of moral value. Ethical intuitionists usually hold that we recognise our duties in the specific features of particular moral decisions.

■ **invalid**
deductively ineffective.

■ **irony**
use of language to convey something entirely different from its literal meaning. Thus, Socrates professed an igno-

rance that was the mark of true wisdom and Kierkegaard often tried to provoke his readers by writing exactly the opposite of what he intended for them to believe.

■ irrelevant conclusion (ignoratio elenchi)

reasoning that misses the point. The informal fallacy of defending the truth of a proposition by appeal to an argument that is actually concerned with something else. Example: 'Parents with large incomes can buy lots of things for their children. Therefore, the children of wealthy parents are happy.'

■ • ism

a general suffix commonly used to designate varieties of philosophical opinion. Although useful for some purposes, such labels should not be taken too seriously. Individual philosophers nearly always deal creatively with complex specific issues, developing arguments in defence of their own views. It is only later that we who read them find it convenient to invent simple names for positions that several of them seem to share. Study of philosophy benefits more from careful reading of the texts themselves than from the artificial classification of their themes.

■ Jansenism

theological belief that obedience to divine will is possible only for those on whom God has already chosen to bestow grace, leaving no room for the exercise of human freedom. This view was originated by Dutch bishop Cornelius Jansen (1585-1638) and defended against Jesuit attacks by members of the Port-Royal community, including Arnauld and Pascal.

■ joint method of agreement and difference

one of Mill's Methods for the discovery of a causal relationship. If an antecedent circumstance is invariably present when, but only when, a phenomenon occurs, it may be inferred to be the cause of that phenomenon.

joint occurrence
the complex event comprising the occurrence of both of its constituent events. The probability of a joint occurrence is calculated by the formula: $P(A \cdot B) = P(A) \times P(B, \text{if } A)$. Thus, for example, the chances of getting 'heads' both times on two tosses of a coin are equal to the chances of getting 'heads' on the first toss (1/2) times the chances of getting 'heads' on the second toss (1/2) or ¼.

judgement (Ger. Urteil)
the mental act of affirming a proposition or the capacity for distinguishing truth from falsity.

just war theory
the attempt to provide acceptable conditions for international conflict. As developed by Augustine and Aquinas, just war theory typically distinguishes the conditions under which war may be intitiated, including a legitimate authority exercising a right intention in pursuit of a just cause, from the rules under which war may be conducted, including concern with proportionality of the means and discrimination between combatants and non-combatants.

justice (Gk. dikh [díkê]; Lat. iustitia)
equitable distribution of goods and evils, including reward and punishment. After surveying alternative notions of the virtue of justice, Plato defined it as the harmonious function of diverse elements of society or of the distinct souls within an individual person. Most social philosophers of the Western tradition, however, have followed Aristotle's conceptions of retributive and distributive justice.

justification
what is offered as grounds for believing an assertion. Hence, also an explanation of the le-

gitimacy of each step in the formal proof of the validity of a deductive argument.

■ Kant, Immanuel (1724-1804)

German philosopher who revolutionised modern philosophy, in an effort to counter the sceptical arguments of Hume and provide a firm basis for human knowledge and morality. Kant used transcendental arguments to show that human beings apply synthetic a priori judgements as the preconditions for any possible experience.

■ kinhsiV (kinêsis)

Greek term for motion or change, a subject of great controversy among Greek philosophers. The Milesians took the facts of change and motion for granted until the Eleatics argued that motion of any kind is impossible. The atomists nevertheless supposed that change is a natural feature of all things. Aristotle argued that every change must be produced by some cause and regarded kinhsiV as the actualisation of some potentiality in the individual substance.

■ knowledge (Gk. gnwsiV [gnôsis], Lat. cognitio, Ger. Wissen)

justified true belief. Since Plato, nearly all Western philosophers have accepted this deceptively simple statement of the three necessary (and jointly sufficient) conditions for knowledge. That is, I know a proposition if and only if: I sincerely affirm the proposition, the prposition is true and my affirmation is genuinely based upon its truth. The correct analysis of each element of the definition, however, is open to question. Philosophers have held different views about the nature of belief and have proposed many different theories of truth.

■ knowledge, theoretical (Gk. episthmh [epistêmê], Lat. scientia)
an organised body of learning, the ultimate aim of human study for many classical philosophers.

■ laissez-faire
French vocative phrase meaning 'Allow to do!' Hence, in political philosophy and economics, a presumption against the desirability of governmental interference with the natural order of society, in general, and with the conduct of free trade, in particular.

■ legal positivism
belief that the laws of a society express nothing other than the will of the sovereign that legislates them. Thus, in opposition to natural law theory, legal positivist John Austin denied that the law is grounded upon any higher morality.

■ lexical definition
a faithful report of the way in which a term is used within a particular language-community.

■ lex talionis
Latin phrase meaning, 'law of retaliation'. Hence, a strictly retributive notion of punishment, according to which anyone who causes injury to another should suffer exactly the same injury in return.

■ liar, paradox of the
the sentence 'I am now lying' would seem to be true (because I am lying) only in those cases when it is false (since what I say is the case) and false (because I am not lying) when it is true (since what I say is not the case). Less personally, the statement 'This sentence is not true' generates a similar perplexity. These are particular instances of the self-referential semantic paradoxes that have troubled logicians since Epimenides, the Cretan who is supposed to have said, "All Cretans are liars."

■ libertas
Latin word for freedom.

locutionary act
the simple speech act of generating sounds that are linked together by grammatical conventions, so as to say something meaningful. Among speakers of English, for example, 'It is raining' performs the locutionary act of saying that it is raining, as 'Grablistrod zetagflx dapu' would not.

logic
branch of philosophy concerned with the distinction between correct and incorrect reasoning. It commonly comprises both deductive and inductive arguments.

logical form
the structure of a proposition or an argument from which all content has been removed. Tautology and validity are features that hold only in virtue of logical form.

logical positivism
twentieth-century philosophical movement that used a strict principle of verifiability to reject as meaningless the non-empirical statements of metaphysics, theology and ethics. Under the influence of Hume, Russell and the early Wittgenstein, the logical positivists regarded as meaningful only statements reporting empirical observations, taken together with the tautologies of logic and mathematics. Prominent logical positivists included members of the Vienna Circle and Ayer.

logicisation of arithmetic
the program conceived by Dedekind, Peano, Frege and Hilbert, but completed by Russell and Whitehead in Principia Mathematica (1913), of showing that arithmetical knowledge can be demonstrated upon the basis of purely logical axioms and definitions. The project was effectively demolished by Gödel's proof that some true formal propositions must nevertheless remain undecidable within the system.

■ logos/muqos (logos / mythos)

Plato's Greek distinction between two ways of explaining what happens: either by providing an explicit rational account (logos), which combines with belief to form accurate knowledge of the essence of things or merely by telling a story with figurative significance (muqos). The Stoics elevated logos into an active principle that generates the specific 'seminal reasons' from which individual things flow. Philo Judaeus fully personified this notion as the divine agent responsible for creation of the world.

■ Lombard, Peter (1095-1160)

Italian theologian and philosopher whose Sententiac in quattuor libris distinctae (Four Books of Sentences) (1158) compiled the assertions and arguments of ancient philosophers and patristic theologians, providing a traditional background upon which late mediaeval scholasticism frequently commented.

■ Machiavelli, Niccolo (1469-1527)

Italian politician and philosopher who offered practical suggestions for the successful use of power, for the achievement of desirable political stability by the arbitrary ruler of any principality, without concern for abstract moral judgements.

■ magnanimity (Gk. megaloyucia [megalopsychía])

greatness of soul. One of Aristotle's most important virtues.

■ major premise

in a categorical syllogism, the premise whose terms are the syllogism's major term and middle term.

■ major term

the predicate term of the conclusion of a categorical syllogism.

Manichaeanism
Persian religion. Followers of Manes (216-277) adhered to a radical dualism between good and evil, or spirit and body, and recommended an ascetic way of life. Augustine, who had been a Manichaean before his conversion to Christianity, later wrote an extended refutation of this heretical doctrine.

material cause
basic stuff of which a thing is made. One of Aristotle's four causes.

material equivalence
the logical relationship between any two propositions that have the same truth-value.

material implication
the logical relationship between any two propositions such that either the first is false or the second is true.

materialism
belief that only physical things truly exist. Materialists claim (or promise) to explain every apparent instance of a mental phenomenon as a feature of some physical object.

matter
physical stuff, whatever has size and shape, is solid and tangible, takes up space, and can move. Hence, for many philosophers of the Western tradition, material objects are substances that have the attribute of extension. Idealists deny the reality of any such stuff, while materialists deny that there is anything else.

mauvaise foi
Sartre's French term for 'bad faith', the culpable self-deception involved in declining to accept responsibility for one's choices.

maximin (or minimax) principle
supposition that the preferable alternative is one whose worst outcome is least harmful, originally in mathematical and game-theoretical contexts. Thus, when success in any venture is uncertain, it is better to choose courses of action that risk the least, even if they don't offer a chance at the most. Rawls argued that this maximisation of the minimum gain to be achieved is a rational guide for social decision-making.

mean (Gk. mesoV [mesos])
the middle way between too much and too little of some-

thing. Aristotle held that virtue is always a mean between vicious extremes of excess and deficiency.

■ **meaning**
the customary significance attached to the use of a word, phrase or sentence, including both its literal sense and its emotive associations. That which is elucidated in a definition. Philosophical theories of meaning endeavour to explain the conditions under which an expression comes to have internal significance and external reference.

■ **mechanism**
belief that science can explain all natural phenomena in terms of the causal interactions among material particles, without any reference to intelligent agency or purpose. As employed by Descartes and Hobbes, mechanism offered an alternative to the scholastic reliance on explanatory appeals to final causes.

■ **megaloyucia (megalopsychia)**
Greek term for magnanimity or greatness of soul, one of the greatest of the moral virtues in the ethics of Aristotle.

■ **meme**
a self-replicating unit of cultural meaning, as understood by biologist Richard Dawkins. Transmitted socially among individuals of different generations, memes evolve through processes of mutation and natural selection. Thus, for example, the jingles sung by children while skipping rope, the conventional standards for fashionable dress and the notions comprising the 'common-sense' view of the world, are all passed on through time, gradually modifying without any deliberate guidance.

■ **memory**
the capacity to recall past experience or information in the present. The reliability of

memory as a source of knowledge and the extent of its contribution to personal identity are matters of philosophical dispute.

■ mens

Latin term for mind.

■ mention

reference to an expression considered merely as a unit of language.

■ mesoV (mesos)

Greek term for middle or mean. The Pythagoreans regarded a balance between extremes as part of the harmonious life proper for human conduct. Aristotle argued more specifically that virtue in human life invariably emerges as the mean between vicious extremes.

■ meta-ethics

branch of philosophical ethics concerned with the meaning of moral propositions and the grounds upon which moral judgements are to be justified. Meta-ethical theories typically offer an account of moral language and its uses, together with an explanation of the logical relations between assertions of fact and value.

■ meta-narrative

stories employed to legitimise the mechanisms of social control. Thus, for example, when parents tell their children, 'We only want to help you avoid our mistakes', they are constructing a meta-narrative that justifies the imposition of rules of conduct they are unwilling to follow themselves.

■ meta-philosophy

branch of philosophy that tries to determine the proper aims, methods and conditions for the discipline of philosophy itself.

■ metaphysics

branch of philosophy concerned with providing a comprehensive account of the most general features of reality as a whole, the study of being as such. Questions about the existence and nature of minds, bodies, God, space, time, causality, unity, identity and the world are all metaphysical issues. From Plato onwards, many philosophers have tried to determine what kinds of things (and how many of each) exist. But Kant argued that this task is impossible. He proposed instead that we consider the general structure of our thought about the world. Strawson calls the former activity revisionary and the latter descriptive, metaphysics.

■ microcosm

literally, a 'little world'. In the philosophy of the Stoics, many neo-platonists and Leibniz, individual human beings are taken to reflect the structure of the universe as a whole.

■ middle term

the term that occurs in both premises (but not in the conclusion) of a categorical syllogism.

■ Milesians

pre-socratic philosophers at Miletus, including Thales, Anaximander and Anaximenes, who speculated about the fundamental principle that unifies the composition of the world.

■ Mill's Methods

patterns of inductive inference elaborated by John Stuart Mill, for the purpose of understanding the grounds upon which it is appropriate to make judgements about causal relationships. The five methods include:

§ the Method of Agreement.
§ the Method of Difference
§ the Joint Method of Agreement and Difference
§ the Method of Residues.
§ the Method of Concomitant Variation.

■ mimhsiV (mimêsis)

Greek term for imitation or representation. Hence, for Plato, mimhsiV is one of the ways in which sensible particulars copy the eternal forms. Thus, he criticised the arts as doubly removed from ultimate reality. Although Aristotle rejected the theory of forms, he agreed with Plato that aesthetic experience is fundamentally mimetic.

■ mind (Gk. nouV [nous]; Lat. mens)
that which thinks, reasons, perceives, wills and feels. Philosophy of mind is concerned with explaining the characteristic features of mental events, the proper analysis of conscious experience, the relation between mind and body, and the moral status of persons.

■ mind-body problem
the difficulty of explaining how the mental activities of human beings relate to their living physical organisms. Historically, the most commonly accepted solutions have included mind-body dualism (Descartes), reductive materialism (Hobbes) or idealism (Berkeley), and the double aspect theory (Spinoza).

■ minor premise
in a categorical syllogism, the premise whose terms are the syllogism's minor term and middle term.

■ minor term
the subject term of the conclusion of a categorical syllogism.

■ misericordiam, argumentum ad
literally, an appeal to 'distress of the heart'.

■ moderation (Gk. swfrosunh [sophrosúnê])
self-control. According to Plato, a person who has the virtue of moderation subordinates the desire for pleasure to the dictates of reason. For Aristotle, all virtues are to be understood as the mean between vicious extremes.

■ Modus Ponens (M.P.)
a rule of inference of the form:

p É q
p
———
q

Example: 'If Tuesday is the 14th, then Friday must be the 17th. Tuesday is the 14th. Therefore, Friday is the 17th.' A simple truth-table shows the validity of this pattern of reasoning.

■ Modus Tollens (M.T.)
a rule of inference of the form:

p É q

$\sim q$

$\sim p$

Example: 'If it had rained this morning, then the grass would still be wet. But the grass is not wet. Therefore, it did not rain this morning.'

A simple truth-table shows that any argument of this form must be valid.

monad

a complete individual substance in the philosophies of Conway and Leibniz, who supposed that each contains all of its properties: past, present and future.

monism

belief that only things of a single kind exist. In its most extreme form, monism may lead to Spinoza's conviction that only a single being is real or the idealist's supposition that everything is comprised by the Absolute. Contemporary philosophers more commonly suppose that many distinct things exist, each of them exhibiting both mental and physical properties.

mood and figure

a unique description of the logical form of a categorical syllogism. The mood lists the forms of its three categorical propositions (in standard form order), while the figure indicates the position of its middle term.

Moore, G. E. (1873-1958)

English philosopher who developed the practice of philosophical analysis as a method for preserving the dictates of common sense against the absurd claims of professional philosophers.

moral / non-moral

distinction between types of value, judgements or propositions. Although a precise line is difficult to draw, there seems to be a genuine difference between universalisable moral concerns that impinge upon other people and merely personal matters of taste. For example:

'Murder is wrong.' is a moral assertion, but.

'This coffee is good.' is a non-moral assertion.

moral argument
an attempt to prove the existence of God, by appeal to presence of moral value in the universe. The fourth of Aquinas's five ways concludes that God must exist as the most perfect cause of all lesser goods. Kant argued that postulation of God's existence is a necessary condition for our capacity to apply the moral law.

moral sense
a putatively innate human faculty for distinguishing right from wrong. In the moral intuitionism of Shaftesbury and Hutcheson, the moral sense motivates proper conduct by enabling us to perceive the distinctive pleasure of moral rectitude.

morfh (morphê)
Greek word for the shape or figure of a thing. Hence, for Aristotle, the fundamental cause which, in conjunction with 'ulh [hylê], constitutes a natural object as a hylomorphic composite.

muqos (mythos)
Greek term for a speech, tale or story, as opposed to a rational explanation.

mysticism
belief in direct apprehension of divine or eternal reality, by means of spiritual contemplation, distinct from more ordinary avenues of human knowledge.

natural law theory
belief that the principles of human conduct can be derived from a proper understanding of human nature in the context of the universe as a rational whole. Although voluntarists suppose that God could will anything at all, Aquinas held that even the divine will is conditioned by reason. Thus, the natural law provides a non-revelatory basis for all human social conduct. Modern appeals to natural law are the foundation for social thought in Grotius and Pufendorf.

naturalism
belief that all objects, events and values can be wholly explained in terms of factual

and/or causal claims about the world, without reference to supernatural powers or authority. Prominent naturalists include Clifford and Dewey. Quine proposed a naturalistic epistemology, understood as empirical study of the origins and uses of sensory information.

■ **naturalistic fallacy**

according to G. E. Moore, the mistake of identifying moral good with any natural property. Moore argued that since any such identification gives rise to an open question, it can never be correct. This constitutes a significant reason for concluding that fact and value remain irreducibly distinct.

■ **necessary / contingent**

distinction between kinds of truth. Necessary truth is a feature of any statement that it would be contradictory to deny. (Contradictions themselves are necessarily false.) Contingent truths (or falsehoods) happen to be true (or false), but might have been otherwise. Thus, for example: 'Squares have four sides.' is necessary.
'Stop signs are hexagonal.' is contingent.
'Pentagons are round.' is contradictory.

■ **necessary / sufficient**

distinction between logical or causal conditions. In logic, one proposition is a necessary condition of another when the second cannot be true while the first is false, and one proposition is a sufficient condition for another when the first cannot be true while the second is false. Thus, for example: 'I have a dog' is a necessary condition for 'My dog has fleas' and 'You scored ninety-five percent' is a sufficient condition for 'You received an A'.

■ **negating the antecedent and the consequent**

a fallacy of the form:

p É q

____

~ p É ~ q

Example: 'If my daughter is sixteen, then I am over thirty. Therefore, if my daughter is not sixteen, then I am not over thirty.'

This pattern of reasoning should be distinguished from legitimate cases of Transposition.

negation

denial, hence, a compound statement that is true if and only if its component statement is false.

p	~ p
T	F
F	T

Negations are symbolised here in the form:

~ p

Example: 'It is not the case that Alan is honest.'

negative proposition

a statement whose propositional quality is determined by the assertion that some or all members of one class of things are excluded from membership in some other class. Examples: 'No fish are birds.' and 'Some birds are not geese.'

The first declares that the classes of fish and birds have no common members, while the second maintains that there is at least one member of the class of birds that is excluded from the class of geese.

neikoV (neikos)

Greek term for a quarrel, feud or battle. Hence, in the philosophy of Empedocles, the spirit of discord or strife in constant struggle with the benevolent influence of filia (philia).

neoplatonism

philosophical system developed by Plotinus and others. Nominally derived from Plato's metaphysics, neoplatonic philosophy regards the natural world as a series of emanations from the nature of god. During most of the mediaeval period, this system was the most influential version of Plato's thought.

neo-Thomism

a nineteenth- and twentieth-century movement that attempts to defend the philosophical and theological doctrines of Thomas Aquinas in a contemporary context.

■ **neutral monism**
belief that both mental and physical properties are the features of substances of a single sort, which are themselves ultimately neither mental nor physical. In distinct varieties, neutral monism was defended by James and Russell.

■ **Nihil est in intellectu quod non prius fuerit in sensu**
Latin phrase meaning 'Nothing is in the understanding that was not earlier in the senses'. Hence, the central doctrine of the empiricism of Gassendi, Locke and Mill.

■ **nihilism**
complete rejection of the existence of human knowledge and values or denial of the possibility of making any useful distinctions among things.

■ **nohsiV (nóêsis)**
Greek word for intuition or thinking, the operation of nouV (nous) without benefit of the discursive reasoning that characterises dianoia (diánoia). According to Plato, such awareness represents the highest portion of human knowledge. From this foundation, Plotinus developed a detailed theory about the operation of the human soul in relation to the world. Husserl later appropriated this Greek term in order to emphasise the characteristic intentionality of mental acts.

■ **nominalism**
belief that only particular things exist, as opposed to realism. Nominalists hold that a general term or name {Lat. nomine} is applied to individuals that resemble each other, without the need of any reference to an independently existing universal.

■ **non sequitur**
Latin phrase meaning, 'It does not follow'. The characteristic feature of arguments that fail to provide adequate support for their conclusions, especially those that commit one of the fallacies of relevance.

noncognitivism

a meta-ethical theory according to which moral issues are not subject to rational determination. Dealing with values, not facts, moral assertions are neither true nor false, but merely express attitudes, feelings, desires or demands.

normative ethics

branch of philosophical ethics concerned with developing theories that determine which human actions are right and which are wrong. It is useful to distinguish normative theories according to the way in which they derive moral value from duties or rights: deontological theories hold that actions are intrinsically right or wrong, while consequentialist theories evaluate actions by reference to their extrinsic outcomes. Virtue ethics theories locate the highest moral value in the development of persons.

Norris, John (1657-1711)

English philosopher. In his Essay towards the Theory of an Ideal World, Norris defended the philosophy of Malebranche against the empiricism of Locke.

noumena

things as they are in themselves.

nouV (nous)

Greek term for mind, reason or intellect. Thus, in the philosophy of Anaxagoras, nouV is an organising principle for the universe as a whole. Plato distinguished this cosmic sense from the more ordinary operation of the human soul, in achieving higher knowledge. Aristotle typically regarded nouV as the distinctive faculty involved in the acquisition of general knowledge. As always, Plotinus elevated this into a quasi-divine principle.

'O' proposition

in the traditional notation for categorical logic, a proposition that is both particular and negative. Example: 'Some trees are not evergreens.' Such a proposition affirms that there is at least one tree that is not also an evergreen. Its contradictory is an 'A' proposition with the same subject and predicate terms.

objective/subjective

distinction between propositions or judgements, about the way things are and those about how people think or feel about them. The truth of objective claims is presumed to be entirely independent of the merely personal concerns reflected in subjective expressions, even though it is difficult to draw the distinction precisely. Thus, for example: 'Spinach is green' is objective, while 'I like spinach' is subjective. 'Seventy-three percent of people in Houston don't like spinach', however, seems to be an objective claim about certain subjects.

obligation

that which binds us to act in accordance with duty. Obligatory acts are those one is morally, legally or contractually required to perform. Normative theories usually try to explain the grounds of moral obligation as well as its practical application.

obscurum per obscurius

Latin phrase meaning 'the obscure through the more obscure'. Hence, the flaw in any account that proves more difficult to understand than what it purports to clarify. In this vein, philosophers reflecting upon each other's work sometimes echo Byron's complaint about Coleridge:

'But, like a hawk encumbered with his hood,
Explaining metaphysics to the nation—
I wish he would explain his explanation.'

obversion

the reciprocal relationship between two categorical propositions of opposite quality, such that the predicate term of each is the complement of the predicate term of the other. Obversion is a valid immediate inference for categorical propositions of every form. Thus, for example: All lizards are reptiles and No lizards are non-reptiles, is a legitimate cases of obversion, either member can be substituted for the other.

occasionalism

belief that natural events are not directly related in causation, since both the apparent cause and the apparent effect are, in fact, produced by some third thing (usually divine providence). Geulincx and Malebranche introduced occasionalism as an improved way of reconciling the mechanism with the dualism of Descartes.

oligarchy

literally, rule by the few. Both Plato and Aristotle assumed that the small group most likely to gain control over the governance of a city-state would be those with great wealth.

ontological argument

an attempt to prove the existence of God by a priori reasoning from the content of the concept of God. As formulated by Anselm, the ontological argument begins with a notion of 'that than which nothing greater can be conceived'. Anything that satisfies this concept must exist in reality as well as in thought (since otherwise it would be possible to conceive something greater, one that really exists), hence, God exists.

ontology

branch of metaphysics concerned with identifying, in the most general terms, the kinds of things that actually exist. Thus, the 'ontological commitments' of a philosophical position include both its explicit assertions and its implicit presuppositions about the existence of entities, substances or beings of particular kinds.

open question argument

G. E. Moore's contention that any effort to define the good must fail, since it always remains possible to ask significantly whether or not the proposed definition is actually good.

operationalism

belief that the meaning of scientific terms and concepts is wholly captured by a description of the process that determines their applicability in particular cases. On this view, theoretical entities are merely logical constructs.

■ **opinion (Gk. doxa [dóxa], Lat. sententia)**
acceptance of a proposition despite a lack of the conclusive evidence that would result in certain knowledge of its truth.

■ **optimism**
belief that everything happens for the best (Lat. optimus), the opposite of pessimism. Thus, for example, Leibniz was an optimist who supposed that this is the best of all possible worlds.

■ **ostension**
the attempt to provide a non-linguistic definition of a term by pointing at something to which it applies. Although useful enough for some primitive purposes, ostensive definitions are systematically ambiguous, since they poorly discriminate among things and their temporal features.

■ **ousia (ousia)**
Greek term for being or substance. Thus, in the philosophy of Aristotle, the most crucial of the categories by means of which to describe a natural object.

■ **pacifism**
opposition to war, killing and violence, support for peace (Lat. pax). Pacifism may be defended deontologically as respect for the value of human life, on the consequentialist grounds that the consequences of violence are clearly harmful or personally as a significant component of good character.

■ **panpsychism**
belief that everything in the world has some mental aspect. This view attributes some degree of consciousness, however small, even to apparently inert bits of matter. Varieties of panpsychism have been defended by the Pythagoreans, Plotinus, Leibniz, Schopenhauer and Whitehead.

■ **pantheism**
belief that God is present in all of nature, rather than transcending it. Spinoza's identification of God with Nature ('Deus sive Natura') and Hegel's notion of the Abso-

lute as World-Spirit are usually regarded as forms of pantheism.

■ **paradigm**

an exemplary instance or model, hence, also, a set of background assumptions. Thus, a 'paradigm case' argument shows that an adequate philosophical analysis must conform to the most ordinary applications of what it analyses. According to Kuhn, procedural paradigms control our study of the natural world during periods between scientific revolutions.

■ **paradox**

an absurd truth. Hence, the derivation of an unacceptable conclusion from apparently unquestionable premises by an apparently valid inference. Resolution of a paradox requires that we abandon at least one of the premises, refute the process of inference or somehow learn to live with the unpalatable result. Zeno used paradoxes to demonstrate the impossibility of motion. Modern semantic paradoxes (such as the liar and the term 'heterological') arise from difficulties inherent in self-reference.

■ **parallelism, psycho-physical**

belief that even though the minds and bodies of human beings are distinct substances that can never interact with each other causally, it is nevertheless true that their development, features and actions coordinate perfectly. Leibniz supposed that this happens as a result of a providentially pre-established harmony.

■ **paronymous**

related though different use of an expression. See **homonymous / synonymous / paronymous**.

■ **parsimony, law of**

belief that the simplest answer is most likely to be the correct one. As a methodological principle, this may be no more than an initial bias in favour of uncomplicated solutions. Its ontological form, that we ought never to multiply entities without necessity, is also known as Ockham's razor.

particular proposition

a statement whose propositional quantity is determined by the assertion that at least one member of one class of things is either included or excluded as a member of some other class. Examples: 'Some cows are Jerseys.' and 'Some school holidays are not postal holidays.' are both particular.

patriarchy

literally, 'rule by the father', hence, any social or political system that grants privileged status to males and permits or encourages their domination of females. Most Western cultures have been, and continue to be, patriarchal in this sense.

perception

awareness of an object of thought, especially that of apparently external objects through use of the senses. Since things don't always turn out actually to be as they seem to us, there is ample reason to wonder about the epistemological reliability of sense perception and theories of perception offer a variety of responses. The sceptical challenge to direct realism is often answered by representative realism, phenomenalism or idealism.

perceptual illusion

cases in which what we apprehend by sensation does not correspond with the way things really are. Thus, for example, the apparent discontinuity between the portions of a spoon in and out of a glass of water is a visual illusion caused by the different indices of refraction of water and air. Representationalists commonly try to account for such cases by appeal to the distinction between primary and secondary qualities, but sceptics and idealists use perceptual illusion to raise more general doubts about the reliability of sensory knowledge.

perfectibility

the Enlightenment belief that proper employment of reason will result in the full achievement of human potential. To various degrees, this optimistic supposition was held by Godwin, Rousseau, Saint-

Simon, Kant, Hegel, Comte and Marx.

■ performative utterance
a linguistic expression used to do something. When spoken by someone in an appropriate position: 'I'm sorry.' makes an apology; 'Play ball!' begins a baseball game and 'I now declare you husband and wife.' performs a marriage. Thus, performatives are important instances of what Austin later called illocutionary acts.

■ Peripatetics
Greek philosophers who followed the principles of Aristotle, so-named because they learned from the master while strolling about in the covered walkways of the Lyceum.

■ perlocutionary act
the speech act of having an effect on those who hear a meaningful utterance. By telling a ghost story late at night, for example, one may accomplish the cruel perlocutionary act of frightening a child.

■ per se / per accidens
Latin phrases meaning 'through itself' and 'by accident', used by medieval philosophers to distinguish essential and accidental features of substances.

■ person
an individual capable of moral agency. Although the details of their theories of human nature differ widely, Descartes, Locke, Kant and Strawson, all accepted a functional description of the person that includes both mental and physical features: the attribution of responsibility to a moral agent requires both the ability to choose and an ability to act on that choice.

■ personal identity
the persistent identity of persons is a matter of special concern for both moral decision-making and the imposition of moral sanctions that are fair and effective. Under

what criteria may we be sure of the identity of the moral agent at different times? Locke proposed a theory of personal identity based on self-conscious appropriation of past and future events. More recently, many philosophers have pointed out the difficulty of establishing the identity of persons independently of their bodily continuity.

■ persuasive definition
an effort to influence attitudes by surreptitiously attaching emotive significance to the meaning of a term. According to Stevenson, the most common instance is an effort to change the descriptive meaning of an emotionally charged evaluative term.

■ pessimism
belief that things generally happen for the worst, the opposite of optimism. Thus, for example, Schopenhauer was a pessimist who supposed that life is endless suffering.

■ petitio principii
the fallacy of circular reasoning.

■ phenomenalism
belief that the immediate objects of sensation provide no evidence for the existence of anything beyond themselves. Taken together with basic principles of empiricism, this entails that what we usually describe as physical objects have no reality apart from our individual, private perceptual experiences of them. Although an anticipation of this view may occur in the work of Berkeley, Mill and most of the logical positivists explicitly defended some form of phenomenalism.

■ phenomenology
description of experience. Hence, a philosophical method restricted to careful analysis of the intellectual processes, of which we are introspectively aware, without making any assumptions about their supposed causal connections to existent external objects. Philosophers who have made extensive use of diverse phenomenological methods include Brentano, Husserl, Hartmann, Heidegger and Merleau-Ponty.

■ phenomena/noumena
Kant's distinction between things as they appear to us and things as they are in themselves. Although cautious application of transcendental arguments may provide a firm basis for knowledge of the former, Kant supposed, the latter lie forever beyond our grasp.

■ philosophy (Gk. filosofia [philosophia])
literally, love of wisdom. Hence, careful thought about the fundamental nature of the world, the grounds for human knowledge and the evaluation of human conduct. As an academic discipline, philosophy's chief branches include logic, metaphysics, epistemology and ethics, and the appropriate aims and methods of each are the concern of metaphilosophy.

■ physicalism
belief that all mental properties, states and events can be wholly explained in terms of physical properties, states and events. Versions of this position, usually focussed on type rather than token identity, predominate in contemporary application of materialist principles to the philosophy of mind.

■ pistiV (pístis)
most general Greek term for belief or faith as a subjective state. According to Plato, this occupies a higher part of the lower portion of the divided line.

■ pity, appeal to (argumentum ad misericordiam)
the informal fallacy that tries to elicit feelings of mercy from an audience.

■ Planck, Max Karl Ernst Ludwig (1858-1947)
German physicist whose discovery of the constant rate at which energy can be radiated contributed significantly to Einstein's formulation of a wave/particle theory of light

and the development of quantum mechanics. Planck won the Nobel Prize in 1918.

■ Plato (427-347 BCE)

Greek philosopher who drew a strict distinction between appearance and reality, developed the theory of forms as an account of immutable truth, and argued that only the wisest members of a society should be trusted to rule.

■ plenitude, principle of

belief that everything that can be, is. Leibniz clearly maintained that every genuine possibility must be actualised in the best of all possible worlds, and A. O. Lovejoy supposed adherence to this notion a significant source for the notion of the great chain of being envisioned by such philosophers as Plato, Plotinus and the Neoplatonics.

■ pluralism

belief that reality ultimately includes many different kinds of things. Thus, in ethics, the supposition that there are many independent sources of values and, in political life, acceptance of a multiplicity of groups with competing interests. Epistemological pluralism is a common feature in post-modernist thought.

■ pneuma (pneuma)

Greek term for wind, breath or spirit. Aristotle relied on the literal senses of the term, but the Stoics gave it a quasi-divine cosmological significance. Hence, pneumatology is the study of spiritual beings, the branch of Christian theology concerned with third person of the trinity.

■ poihsiV (poiêsis)

Greek term for creation or production that is aimed at some end, unlike mere action or doing. Excellence in poihsiV is achieved by skill tecnh [technê].

Polish notation

an alternative representation for symbolic logic, introduced by Jan Lukasiewicz. Use of the basic notation is illustrated in the following table:

Np negation ~ p

Kpq conjunction p · q

Apq disjunction p Ú q

Cpq material implication p É q

Epq material equivalence p º q

PxFx universal quantifier (x) Fx

SxGx existential quantifier ($x)Gx

Polish notation eliminates any need for parenthetical bracketing by relying upon a rigorous principle of order. Thus, for example,

{(pÚr) ·[(pÉ~q) ·(rÉs)]} É(~qÚs).

can be expressed in Polish notation as CKAprKCpNqCrs ANqs.

politics

what pertains to the life of the city or state. Hence, study of citizenship or the art of governance generally. Political philosophers, including Plato, Aristotle, Machiavelli, Hobbes, Locke, Rousseau, Mill, Marx and MacKinnon examine the origins, forms and limits of political power as exercised in practical life.

populum, argumentum ad

an attempt to persuade by reference to commonplace sentiments.

Porphyry (232-304)

Phoenecian philosopher. A disciple of Plotinus, Porphyry defended the neo-platonic philosophy in Peri agalmaton (On Images) and several commentaries on the logic of Aristotle, including an influential exposition of the Categories.

Port-Royal

monastery outside Paris that fostered Jansenism during the seventeenth century. During its heyday, Port-Royal hosted Antoine Arnauld (whose sister Angélique was its abbess),

Pierre Nicole, and Blaise Pascal, along with Jean Racine.

■ **positivism**

belief that natural science, based on observation, comprises the whole of human knowledge. Positivists like Auguste Comte, reject as meaningless the claims of theology and metaphysics. The most influential twentieth-century version is logical positivism.

■ **post hoc, ergo propter hoc**

Latin phrase meaning 'After this, therefore because of this'. Thus, mistaken reliance upon temporal succession alone as enough to establish the presence of a causal relationship between two events.

■ **postulate**

a proposition assumed to be true, without any appeal to evidentiary support, especially when it is used to derive further statements in a formal system or general theory.

■ **potentiality (Gr. dunamiV [dynamis])**

what might have been or could be, as opposed to what is the case. Hence, for Aristotle, a disposition or tendency to manifest itself.

■ **pragmatic theory of truth**

belief that a proposition is true when acting upon it yields satisfactory practical results. As formulated by William James, the pragmatic theory promises (in the long term) a convergence of human opinions upon a stable body of scientific propostions, that have been shown, in experience, to be successful principles for human action.

pragmatism
an indigenous American philosophical theory that explains both meaning and truth in terms of the application of ideas or beliefs to the performance of actions that have observable practical outcomes. Prominent pragmatists in the tradition include Peirce, James, Mead, Addams and Dewey.

praxiV (praxis)
Greek term for action or doing, as opposed to creative production. According to Aristotle, actions are subject to moral valuation, if they result from deliberate choice.

precising definition
a careful effort to reduce the vagueness of a term by stipulating features not included in its lexical definition.

predicate calculus
a formal logical system constructed to symbolise assertions that individual things have such features.

predicate constant
a symbol (usually uppercase letters such as F, G, H, etc.) used to represent a specific feature or property in quantification theory.

prediction
the explanation of an event that has not yet occurred, by reference to observed regularities in the natural world.

premise
a statement whose truth is used to infer that of others.

prescriptivism
R. M. Hare's contention that the use of moral language conveys an implicit commitment to act accordingly. Thus, for example, saying that 'Murder is wrong' not only entails acceptance of a universalisable obligation not to kill, but also leads to avoidance of the act of killing.

pre-socratic philosophers
Greek philosophers of the sixth and fifth centuries B.C.E., many of them known to us only through fragmentary reports by later writers, whose speculative and practical thought predates the development of critical philosophy by Socrates and Plato. Prominent pre-socratics include: Thales, Anaximander,

Anaximenes, Pythagoras, Heraclitus, Xenophanes, Parmenides, Zeno of Elea, Empedocles, Anaxagoras, Protagoras, Hippias, Leucippus, Democritus and the Sophists.

■ **presupposition**

what is implicitly involved in making an assertion. Hence, according to P.F. Strawson, a presupposition is a necessary condition for either the truth or the falsity of the statement that presupposes it. Thus, for example, 'My grand-daughter is a smart baby', whether or not she exhibits intelligent behaviour, presupposes that I do, in fact, have at least one female grand-child.

■ **Price, Henry Habberly (1899-1984)**

British philosopher who defended a comprehensive theory of the relation between sense-data and material objects in Perception (1932), Hume's Theory of the External World (1946) and Thinking and Experience (1953).

■ **Prichard, H. A. (1871-1947)**

English philosopher whose posthumously-published essays influenced a generation of Oxford philosophers. Prichard defended moral intuitionism in 'Does Moral Philosophy Rest on a Mistake?' (1921) and Moral Obligation (1949). Price also offered support for perceptual realism in Knowledge and Perception (1950).

■ **prima facie**

Latin phrase meaning 'at first sight'. Thus, in the ethics of W. D. Ross, a prima facie duty is a defeasible presumption that we are obligated to perform an action.

■ **primary/secondary qualities**

distinction between perceived aspects of things. The primary qualities are intrinsic features of the thing itself (its size, shape, internal structure, mass and momentum, for example), while the secondary qualities are merely its powers to produce sensations in us (its colour, odour, sound and taste, for example). This distinction was carefully drawn by Galileo, Descartes, Boyle and Locke, whose statement of the distinction set the tone for future scientific inquiry. But Foucher, Bayle and Berkeley argued that the distinction is groundless, so that all sensible qualities exist only in the mind of the perceiver.

private language argument

Wittgenstein's contention that it is impossible for an isolated individual to employ language, since a single person could not have adequate criteria for following linguistic rules. This argument is commonly taken as a refutation of solipsism.

probability

the likelihood that an event will occur, expressed quantitatively by a number ranging from 0 (impossible) to 1 (certain). Initial probabilities are often assigned either on the classical assumption that every possible outcome is equally likely to occur or by careful empirical observation of the relative frequency with which events have actually occurred in the past. The likelihood of alternative and joint occurrences can be calculated directly from these initial values.

problematic / assertoric / apodeictic

distinction among the modalities of propositions. A problematic proposition states what is possible, an assertoric proposition states what is actual and an apodeictic proposition states what is necessary. For example: 'A novel could be larger than a dictionary.' is problematic. 'Atlanta is larger than Knoxville.' is assertoric.

'142 is larger than 37.' is apodeictic.

■ proof

a formal demonstration of the validity of a deductive argument.

■ proposition

what is conveyed by a declarative sentence used to make a statement or assertion. Each proposition is either true or false, though, in a particular instance, we may not know which it is.

■ propositional calculus

a formal system of symbolic logic concerned with compound statements formed by the use of truth-functional logical connectives.

■ Protagoras of Abdera (485-415 BCE)

presocratic philosopher, one of the sophists. Protagoras is best known for the relativistic assertion that human beings are 'the measure of all things'.

■ prudence (Gk. fronhsiV [phrónêsis]; Lat. prudentia)

practical wisdom, sound judgement in everyday life, as distinguished from theoretical wisdom. According to Aristotle, this ability to discover and carry out the proper goals of human life is a vital element in moral deliberation.

■ yuch (psychê)

Greek term for soul as the essential principle of life and the locus of consciousness. Although used pre-philosophically, simply in reference to the 'breath of life', the term was associated by pre-socratic philosophers, including especially Anaxagoras, with an explanatory principle. Pythagorean thought proposed that the yuch be understood as the persistent element in the life of an individual. Plato expanded upon this view with a detailed account of the tripartate soul, with associated human virtues and an argument for the immortality of its rational component. Aristotle restored a broader sense of the term, using it for the several functions characteristic of living things generally. Neo-platonic thinkers made it the cosmic principle of all motion.

■ punishment

deliberate infliction of harm, as a moral sanction against offenders. Punishment may be understood, designed and applied according to any of the three major varieties of normative theory: retribution and reparation focus on satisfaction of duties, deterrence and prevention on securing desirable outcomes, and reform and rehabilitation on improving moral character.

■ Q.E.D. (quod erat demonstrandum)

Latin for 'what was to be proven'. Hence, a common way of identifying the conclusion of a mathematical or logical argument. (It doesn't really mean 'Quite Easily Done'.).

■ qualia

the intrinsic phenomenal features of subjective consciousness or sense data. Thus, qualia include what it is like to see green grass, to taste salt, to hear birds sing, to have a headache, to feel pain, etc. Providing an adequate account of qualia is sometimes held to be a difficult problem for functionalist explanations of mental states.

■ qualities

the properties or features of things, whether they are intrinsic or extrinsic to the thing itself.

■ quality (propositional)

along with propositional quantity, one of the distinguishing features among categorical propositions:

· an affirmative proposition (A or I) states a relation of inclusion between members of the classes designated by its terms.

· a negative proposition (E or O) states a relation of exclusion between members of the classes designated by its terms.

■ quantification rules

valid argument forms, including Universal Instantiation, Universal Generalisation, Existential Instantiation and Existential Generalisation, whose substitution instances may be used to manipulate the use of quantifiers in a formal proof of the validity of a more complex deductive argument.

■ **quantification theory**

the formal system of logic (also known as the predicate calculus) that incorporates the entire propositional calculus and adds a set of quantification rules.

■ **quantifiers**

logical symbols used in the predicate calculus (or quantification theory) to indicate the extent of the application of a propositional function.

The universal quantifier, (x) , indicates that the proposition applies to everything, so that '(x)(Fx É Gx)' may be read as, 'For any x, if x is F then x is G.'

The existential quantifier, ($x) , indicates that the proposition applies to something, so that '($x)(Fx · Gx)' may be read as, 'There is at least one x such that x is F and x is G.'

■ **quantity (propositional)**

along with propositional quality, one of the distinguishing features among categorical propositions:

· a universal proposition (A or E) refers to all members of the class designated by its subject term.

· a particular proposition (I or O) refers only to some members of that class.

■ **quantum mechanics**

a physical theory developed by Planck, Heisenberg and Schrödinger. Quantum theory typically permits only probable or statistical calculation of the observed features of subatomic particles, understood in terms of wave functions.

■ **quaternio terminorum**

Latin name for the fallacy of four terms.

■ **Quine, Willard Van Orman (1908-2000)**

American philosopher. Quine employs the methods of pragmatism and logical positivism in the support of a strict linguistic nominalism. He argued that neither the analytic/synthetic distinction, nor the equivalence of meaning are defensible on strictly empiricist grounds.

■ **rationalism**

reliance on reason as the only reliable source of human knowledge. In the most general application, rationalism offers a naturalistic alternative to appeals to religious accounts of human nature and conduct. More specifically, rationalism is the epistemological theory that significant knowledge of the world can best be achieved by a priori means. It therefore stands in contrast to empiricism.

■ **realism**

belief that universals exist independently of the particulars that instantiate them. Realists hold that each general term signifies a real feature or quality, which is numerically the same in all the things to which that term applies. Thus, opposed to nominalism.

■ **realism, perceptual**

belief that material objects exist independently of our perception of them. (Thus, opposed to idealism.) Realistic theories of perception include both representationalism, in which awareness of objects is mediated by our ideas of them, and direct realism, which presumes an immediate relation between the observer and the observed.

■ **reality (Ger. Wirklichkeit)**

the totality of what is, as opposed to what merely seems to be. Metaphysicians and ontologists differ widely in their convictions about what kinds of entities are properly included.

■ **reason (Ger. Vernunft)**

the intellectual ability to apprehend the truth cognitively, either immediately in intuition or by means of a process of inference.

■ recollection (Gk. anamnhsiV [anámnêsis])

belief that we come to know fundamental truths by recalling our acquaintance with their eternal objects before birth. Plato (perhaps following the lead of Socrates) defended recollection as the source of our knowledge of mathematics and morality in Meno, Phaedo and The Republic.

■ recursive

capable of being indefinitely re-applied to the results of its own application. Hence, a recursive definition is one that begins with one or more initial instances and then specifies the repeatable rules for deriving others. Thus, for example: 'A person's descendants include that person's children and all of their descendants' is a recursive definition (not a circular definition) of the word 'descendant'.

■ reductio ad absurdum

a method of proving that a proposition must be false (or true) by assuming the truth (or falsity) of the proposition and then showing that this assumption, taken together with other premises whose truth is already established, would lead to a contradiction (or, at least, to an obvious falsehood). This method is sometimes called indirect proof.

■ reductionism

belief that statements or expressions of one sort can be replaced systematically by statements or expressions of a simpler or more certain kind. Thus, for example, some philosophers have held that arithmetic can be reduced to logic, that the mental can be reduced to the physical or that the life sciences can be reduced to the physical sciences.

■ redundancy theory of truth

belief that it is always logically superfluous to claim that a proposition is true, since this claim adds nothing further to a simple affirmation of the proposition itself. 'It is true that I am bald.' means the same thing as 'I am bald.'

reference (Ger. Bedeutung)
the relation that holds between a term and the things to which it applies.

Regan, Tom (1938-)
American philosopher. In The Case for Animal Rights (1983) and The Thee Generations Reflections on the Coming Revolution (1991), Regan develops a comprehensive theory in favour of granting moral respect to non-human animals.

Régis, Pierre-Sylvain (1632-1707)
French Cartesian philosopher. Unable to secure an adequate metaphysical defence of mind-body dualism, Regis proposed that the interaction of accidentally conjoined substances can only be accepted on faith.

reification
improperly treating something as if it were an object. In the political thought of Lukacs and other Marxists, reification often involves trying to turn human beings into marketable commodities. The philosophical reification of abstract concepts is commonly called hypostasisation.

relativism
belief that human judgements are always conditioned by the specific social environment of a particular person, time or place. Cognitive relativists hold that there can be no universal knowledge of the world, but only diverse interpretations of it. Moral relativists hold that there are no universal standards of moral value, but only the cultural norms of particular societies.

Renaissance
fourteenth-, fifteenth- and sixteenth-century European intellectual movement, characterised by rejection of scholastic authority, renewed interest in classical antiquity and excitement about the prospect of achieving scientific knowledge. Prominent Renaissance thinkers include Lorenzo Valla, Marsillio Ficino, Giovanni Pico della Mirandola, Desiderius Erasmus, Thomas More, Giordano Bruno and Francisco Suarez.

replacement, rules of
tautologies that express the logical equivalence of pairs of elementary statement forms, each of whose substitution instances may be used to replace those of the other, wherever they occur within a formal proof of the validity of a deductive argument. The rules of replacement that we employ here include: De Morgan's Theorems, Commutation, Association, Distribution, Double Negation, Transposition, Implication, Equivalence, Exportation and Tautology. These, taken together with the nine rules of inference, adequately secure the completeness of the propositional calculus.

representationalism
theory of perception according to which we are aware of objects only through the mediation of the ideas that represent them. Descartes and Locke were both representationalists. Although it handily accounts for perceptual illusion and memory, such a theory often leads (as in Hume) to scepticism about the existence of external objects.

res cogitans / res extensa
Descartes's Latin distinction of the two major ontological categories comprising reality: thinking things and extended things, or minds and bodies.

residues, method of
one of Mill's Methods for discovering causal relationships. If portions of a complex phenomenon can be explained by reference to parts of a complex antecedent circumstance, whatever remains of that circumstance may be inferred to be the cause of the remainder of that phenomenon. Example: 'The old prescription contained vitamins A, B-12 and C, and taking it regularly improved night vision, reduced stress and prevented colds. The new prescription contains calcium along with vitamins A, B-12 and C, and taking it regularly improves night vision, reduces stress, prevents colds and increases bone density. Therefore, taking calcium regularly increases bone density.'

responsibility

accountability for the actions one performs and the consequences they bring about, for which a moral agent could be justly punished or rewarded. Moral responsibility is commonly held to require the agent's freedom to have done otherwise.

Riemann, Georg Friedrich Bernhard (1826-1866)

German mathematician and physicist. Riemann developed field theory as a mathematical description of phenomena as apparently diverse as gravitation, magnetism, electricity and light, and contributed to the development of topology and non-Euclidean geometry.

rights

justified expectations about the benefits other people or society ought to provide. We are entitled to our rights, in the sense that others have a moral obligation to respect them. At an individual level, my duty to act towards you in a certain way entails your corresponding right to my performance of that action.

rigid designator

an expression that refers to the same thing in every possible world. According to Saul Kripke, proper names and terms that signify natural kinds (unlike definite descriptions) designate rigidly, so that we can make counterfactual assertions about their referents, whether or not they exist in our world.

Rohault, Jacques (1620-1672)

French philosopher and physicist, author of System of Natural Philosophy (1667). As a follower of Descartes, Rohault argued that animal behaviour can be explained in purely mechanistic terms. But, unlike many of his fellow Cartesians, he held that in human beings, the mind and the body participate in reciprocal relations of genuine causal interaction.

■ Ross, William David (1877-1971)

British moral philosopher who also produced valuable translations of the philosophical works of Aristotle. In The Right and the Good (1930), Ross criticised the ethical theory of Moore and offered, in its place, an intuitionist theory, giving central importance to the possession of prima facie moral duties to perform certain actions.

■ Rousseau, Jean-Jacques (1712-1778)

Swiss political philosopher who held that the citizens of the state form a collective body, ruled only by the general will that arises from each and applies to all, resulting in perfect freedom and equality.

■ Royce, Josiah (1855-1916)

American philosopher. Royce's subtle reasoning in defence of absolute idealism in The Religious Aspect of Philosophy (1885) and The World and the Individual (1901) fostered (in opposition) the development of pragmatism by James.

■ Ruddick, Sara Loop (1935-)

American philosopher. In Maternal Thinking: Towards a Politics of Peace (1989), Ruddick argues that focus on preserving, fostering and training children has a transformative effect on moral judgement and practice. People who empathise with others, teach the need for interpersonal respect and aim for reconciliation, she argues, can be freed from the violent effects of (masculine) human aggression.

■ rule utilitarianism

view that an action is right, provided that good consequences would follow if everyone acted in the same way.

■ Russell, Bertrand (1872-1970)

English mathematician and philosopher whose work

ranged widely, including attention to formal logic and the philosophy of mathematics, epistemology and metaphysics, and vigorous commitment to unpopular political causes.

■ Ryle, Gilbert (1900-1976)

British philosopher. Ryle proposed a philosophical method of dissolving problems by correctly analysing inappropriate uses of language. By this means, he identified a category mistake at the heart of Cartesian dualism and defended linguistic behaviourism in its place.

■ Saadiah, Gaon (Sa'adyah ben Joseph) (882-942)

Jewish philosopher and linguist who translated classic Hebrew literature into Arabic and offered rational arguments in defence of religious doctrine, in his Sefer ha-Nivhar ha-Emunot ve-D'eol (The Book of Critically Chosen Beliefs and Convictions) (933). According to Saadiah, the destructive force of pleasure in human life can be overcome only by attention to the Torah.

■ Saint-Simon, Comte de (Claude-Henri de Rouvroy) (1760-1825)

French political thinker whose socialism greatly influenced the work of Comte and Marx. Saint-Simon's Du système industriel (On the Industrial System) (1821) acknowledged the functional difference between distinct social classes, decried reliance on a feeble bureaucracy and suggested that the organised state would wither away once economic benefits have been equitably distributed. Letters from an Inhabitant of Geneva (1803) offers a brief statement of several of these notions. Saint-Simon's criticism of traditional religion may be found in Nouveau christianisme (New Christianity) (1825).

■ **salva veritate**

Latin for 'saving the truth'. If two expressions can be interchanged without changing the truth-value of the statements in which occur, they are said to be substitutable salva veritate.

■ **sanction, moral**

an extrinsic force that is supposed to motivate moral agents to perform their duties. Positive and negative sanctions commonly include reward and punishment by the state, praise and blame by other people, and the dictates of one's own conscience. The natural consequences of one's actions are not usually regarded as sanctions.

■ **Santayana, George (1863-1952)**

Spanish-American philosopher who defended the primacy of aesthetic value in human life. In Scepticism and Animal Faith (1923), Santayana argued that all human knowledge derives from an instinctive urge to believe, even though objective truth necessarily lies beyond our capacity. He also wrote the multivolume works, The Life of Reason (1905-6), extolling the unique values of a spiritual appreciation of the universe, and Realms of Being (1927-1940), identifying matter, spirit, essence and truth as his basic categories.

■ **Sartre, Jean-Paul (1905-1980)**

French playwright, novelist and philosopher who proposed an existentialist analysis of the human condition upon which our radical freedom typically produces feelings of anguish, forlornness and despair.

Satyagraha

Sanskrit term (literally, truth-force) used by Gandhi for the practice of non-violence in the face of political oppression.

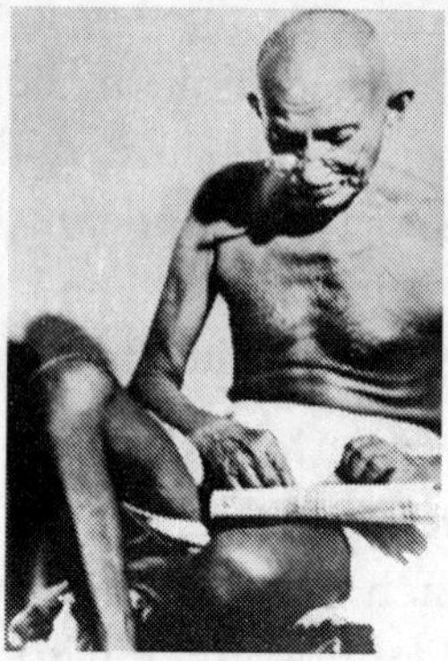

Saussure, Ferdinand de (1857-1913)

Swiss linguist. Saussure's emphasis on the communicative value of language in Cours de linguistique générale (Course in General Linguistics) (1916) constituted the foundation of modern structuralism. According to Saussure, each signifying concept is produced in the context of a system of differences, the range of alternative choices that its user might have employed in its stead. Thus, the meaning of a word has less to do with its referent than with its relation to other words. On this view, the structured language of a society is a closed system whose coherence and generality are independent of what it signifies.

scepticism

belief that some or all human knowledge is impossible. Since even our best methods for learning about the world sometimes fall short of perfect certainty, sceptics argue, it is better to suspend belief than to rely on the dubitable products of reason. Classical sceptics include Pyrrho and Sextus Empiricus. In the modern era, Montaigne, Bayle and Hume, all advocated some form of sceptical philosophy. Fallibilism is a more moderate response to the lack of certainty.

■ Schelling, Friedrich Wilhelm Joseph von (1775-1854)

German philosopher whose System des Transzendentalen Idealismus (System of Transcendental Idealism) (1800) introduced Romantic elements into the development of post-Kantian idealism. Arguing that Fichte's idealism put too much emphasis on the merely subjective individual ego, Schelling proposed a notion of objective transcendental consciousness. His identification of nature with intellect in Darstellung meines Systems der Philosophie (Presentation of my System of Philosophy) (1801) and Vorlesungen über die Methode des akademishen Studiums (Lectures on the Method of Academic Study) (1803) provided a basis from which Hegel would derive the fully considered concept of the Absolute.

■ Schiller, Johann Christoph Friedrich von (1759-1805)

German philosopher and poet who wrote a series of popular 'Sturm und Drang' plays, including Die Räber and Wilhelm Tell. Although he criticised Kant's ethical theory in Über Anmuth und Würde (On Grace and Dignity) (1793), Schiller applied Kantian notions to the sensuous appreciation of aesthetic experience in Briefe über die äesthetische Erziehung des Menschen (Letters on the Aesthetic Education of Man) (1795).

■ scholasticism

Philosophical study as practiced by Christian thinkers in mediaeval universities. The scholastics typically relied upon ancient authorities as sources of dogma and engaged in elaborate disputations over their proper interpretation. These practices were largely discontinued by philosophers of the Renaissance.

■ Schrödinger, Erwin (1887-1961)

Austrian physicist who established modern wave mechanics and employed thought-experiments about the superposition of contradictory states to explore the apparently paradoxical consequences of quantum mechanics. Schrödinger shared the Nobel Prize for Physics in 1933.

■ scientia

Latin term for an organised body of theoretical knowledge.

■ scientific method

a procedure for the development and evaluation of explanatory hypothesis.

■ Scotus, John Duns (1266-1308)

British Franciscan philosopher. Scotus developed the notion of a formal distinction (more than nominal but less than real) as the key to resolving problems of individuation. On this basis, Scotus distinguished intellect from volition and defended freedom of the will against the determinism of the radical Aristoteleans. His Treatise on God as First Principle employs a revision of Anselm's ontological argument in defence of the existence of god.

■ Searle, John (1932-)

American philosopher. Expanding on the work of J.L. Austin, Searle's Speech Acts: An Essay in the Philosophy of Language (1969) treats all communication as instances of the performance of speech acts. In Intentionality: An Essay in the Philosophy of Mind (1983) and The Rediscovery of the Mind (1992), Searle emphasises the irreducibility of consciousness and intentionality to the merely physical elements of human existence. The 'Chinese Room' thought-experiment in his 'Minds, Brains, and Programs' (1980) purports to show that even effective computer simulations do not embody genuine intelligence, since rule-governed processes need not rely upon understanding by those who perform them.

■ secondary qualities

the extrinsic features that things produce in us when we perceive them, as opposed to the primary qualities the things are supposed to have in themselves.

secundum quid
Latin for 'according to something' (in contrast with simpliciter). Hence, a common abbreviation for 'a dicto simpliciter ad dictum secundum quid' and 'a dicto secundum quid ad dictum simpliciter', Latin designations for the informal fallacies of accident and converse accident.

self-deception
avoidance or outright denial of unpleasant aspects of reality, especially those which might otherwise warrant an unfavourable opinion about ourselves. Thus, for example, the wishful thought, 'I'm not really addicted to nicotine, I could quit smoking any time.' is clearly self-deceptive. Kierkegaard, Heidegger, and Sartre condemned self-deception as bad faith or an inauthentic response to the anxiety produced by contemplation of human freedom.

self-evident
certainly known without proof. The notion of self-evidence is commonly assimilated either to that of a priori knowledge or to that of logical tautology.

Sellars, Wilfrid (1912-1989)
American philosopher; author of Science, Perception, and Reality (1963) and Essays in Philosophy and its History (1974). Sellars employed the methods of logical positivism and analytic philosophy to forge a unique account of human knowledge. In 'Empiricism and the Philosophy of Mind' (1956), Sellars tried to develop functional descriptions of human behaviour by means of which to reconcile intentionality with materialism.

semantic theory of truth
belief that any claim that a proposition is true can be made only as a formal requirement regarding the language in which the proposition itself is expressed. Thus, according to Tarski, 'It rained today' is true if and only if it rained today. The distinction

between different levels of language employed by this theory is presumed to offer a convenient evasion of otherwise troublesome semantic paradoxes.

■ semantics
theory of meaning, study of the signification of signs or symbols, as opposed to their formal relations (syntactics).

■ semiotics
theory of signs, comprising both semantics and syntactics, especially in the philosophy of language of Peirce and Saussure.

■ Seneca, Lucius Annaeus (4 B.C.E.-65 C.E.)
Roman statesman whose Epistulae Morales (Moral Letters) and Dialogi (Dialogues) propounded the stoic philosophy, of which his suicide was popularly taken to be an exemplary application.

■ sensation (Gk. aisqhsiV [aisthêsis])
conscious experience or feeling that apparently conveys awareness of the external world. Empiricists commonly suppose that sensations are the basis for our a posteriori knowledge of the world.

■ sense / reference (Ger. Sinn / Bedeutung)
distinction about the meaning of words introduced by Frege. The sense of an expression is the thought it expresses, while its reference is the object it represents. Since the ability to use a term presupposes familiarity with its sense but not knowledge of its reference, statements of identity can be genuinely informative when they link two terms with the same reference but distinct senses, as in 'The husband of Barbara Bush is the President who succeeded Ronald Reagan.'

■ sense data
immediate objects of sensation, also known as sensa or sensibilia, especially in representationalist theories of perception.

■ Seth (Pringle-Pattison), Andrew (1856-1931)
Scottish idealist who regarded the personality of the individual human being as the central unifying element in

the construction of knowledge of reality.

Sextus Empiricus (c. 200)

Ancient sceptic who defended the practical viability of Pyrrhonism as the only way of life that results in genuine ataraxia [ataraxia], in Pyrrhonian Hypotyposeis (Outlines of Pyrrhonism). The translation into Latin of Sextus's comprehensive criticisms of ancient schools of thought in Adversos Mathematicos (Against the Dogmatists), provided an important resource for the development of modern scepticism during the sixteenth century.

Shaftesbury, Third Earl of (Anthony Ashley Cooper) (1671-1713)

English moral essayist. Raised in genteel circumstances by his grandfather, one of the Lords Proprietor of the Carolina colonies and a close associate of Locke, Shaftesbury proposed a set of practical rules for living, that he claimed to arise from the natural dispositions of all human beings, without any reliance on divine revelation, in An Inquiry concerning Virtue or Merit (1699). This was an important step in the development of the notion of a moral sense by Hutcheson and Hume. Shaftesbury's works were collected in Characteristics of Men, Manners, Opinions, and Times (1711).

Sheffer stroke

a truth-functional connective that suffices to symbolise every dyadic relation between statements. Since ‘ p | q ‘ (or ‘not both p and q’) takes the truth-values illustrated in the truth-table at right, negation can be defined as ‘ p | p ’, and disjunction as ‘ (p | p) | (q | q) ’. From these, in turn, all of the other connectives can be derived.

p	q	p | q
T	T	F
T	F	T
F	T	T
F	F	T.

Sidgwick, Henry (1838-1900)

English moral and political philosopher. In The Methods of Ethics (1874) and Outlines of the History of Ethics (1886), Sidgwick surveyed the varieties of argument that may be applied to moral judgements, including intuitive common-sense, calculation of self-interest and a utilitarian normative theory. He supposed that although each is well-founded, the three cannot be wholly reconciled with each other. We are therefore perpetually vulnerable to the possibility of conflicting moral obligations.

■ Siger of Brabant (1235-1282)

French philosopher. As one of the radical Aristoteleans in Paris, Siger endorsed the philosophy of Ibn Rushd and rejected mediaeval preoccupation with theological concerns in his Quaestiones in Metaphysicam (Metaphysical Questions). Suspected of pursuing a 'double truth', Siger became one of the chief targets of the Condemnation of 1270.

■ simpliciter

Latin for 'simply' or 'naturally' (in contrast with secundum quid). Hence, what anything is when considered absolutely or without qualification.

■ Simplification (Simp.)

a rule of inference of the form:

$$\frac{p \cdot q}{p}$$

Example: 'Jevona is tall and Jevona is thin. Therefore, Jevona is tall.' Although trivial in ordinary language, this pattern of reasoning is vital for proof construction in the propositional calculus.

■ sine qua non

Latin for 'without which, not', hence, an alternative way of expressing the presence of a necessary condition.

■ Singer, Peter (1946-)

Australian philosopher. Singer is an ethicist whose Practical

Ethics (1979) emphasises the application of consequentialist moral principles to matters of personal and social concern. He is most widely admired for Animal Liberation (1975), in which Singer shows that, since a difference of species entails no moral distinction between sentient beings, it is wrong to mistreat non-human animals. It follows that animal experimentation and the eating of animal flesh are morally indefensible. In 'Do Animals Feel Pain?, Singer argues for the moral relevance of animal pain.

■ singular proposition

a statement that some individual has a particular feature. In categorical logic, since its subject term designates a unit class, the singular proposition should be interpreted as the conjunction of corresponding universal and particular propositions (either as A and I or as E and O).

■ Sinn / Bedeutung

Frege's German distinction between the sense and reference of a term, intended to account for the possibility of genuinely informative statements of identity.

■ Smart, John Jamieson Carswell (1920-)

English-Australian philosopher. Influenced by the methods of Ryle, Smart defends a strictly physicalist philosophy of mind in Philosophy and Scientific Realism (1963). Smart's noncognitivist approach to morality yields a defence of act utilitarianism in Utilitarianism: For and Against (1973), co-authored with Bernard Williams.

■ Smith, Adam (1723-1790)

Scottish philosopher and economist. Smith modified the moral sense theory, in his Theory of Moral Sentiments (1759), placing greater emphasis than had Hutcheson on the sentiment of sympathy and the virtue of self-control. Smith's An Inquiry into the Nature and Causes of the Wealth of Nations (1776) proposed the economic theory that social goods are maximised when individual human beings are permitted to pursue their own interests, restricted only by the most general principles of justice.

■ social contract theory

belief that political structures and the legitimacy of the state derive from an (explicit or implicit) agreement by individual human beings to surrender (some or all of) their private rights in order to secure the protection and stability of an effective social organisation or government. Distinct versions of social contract theory were proposed by Hobbes, Locke, Rousseau and Rawls.

■ Socrates (470-399 B.C.E.)

Greek philosopher. He was the teacher of Plato, from whom we have our best knowledge of his philosophical methods. Although he wrote nothing, Socrates left Western philosophy the rich legacy of his example in the persistent pursuit of truth.

■ solipsism

belief that only I myself and my own experiences are real, while anything else, a physical object or another person, is nothing more than an object of my consciousness. As a philosophical position, solipsism is usually the unintended consequence of an over-emphasis on the reliability of internal mental states, which provide no evidence for the existence of external referents.

■ sofia [sophía]

Greek term for the intellectual virtue of wisdom, in contrast with the more practical function of fronhsiV (phrónêsis). According to Plato, this is the distinctive feature of rulers in the ideal state and the crowning achievement of the rational soul of an individual.

■ **sophism**

a plausible argument that is actually fallacious, especially when someone dishonestly presents it as if it were legitimate reasoning.

■ **sophists**

pre-socratic philosophers who offered to teach young Athenians how to use logic and rhetoric to defeat opponents in any controversy. Socrates and Plato sharply criticised most of the sophists because they accepted monetary rewards for encouraging unprincipled persuasive methods.

■ **swfrosunh (sôphrosúnê)**

Greek term for moderation, the capacity to exercise self-control over one's desire for pleasure. For Plato, this is the virtue best exemplified by the masses in the ideal state. According to Aristotle, however, swfrosunh is even more crucial, since every moral virtue is properly conceived as the mean between vicious extremes.

■ **sorites**

a complex variety of argument, consisting entirely of categorical syllogisms linked together by the use of the same propositions as the conclusions of some and the premises of others. Example: 'Some pets are cardinals, but all cardinals are finches, while every finch is a bird, and only warm-blooded animals are birds. Hence, some pets are birds.' Applied to vague predicates, such chains of reasoning may result in paradox: if one grain of sand does not make a heap and the addition of a second grain of sand does not make a heap, and the addition of a third grain of sand does not make a heap, etc., etc., then it would seem to follow (contrary to fact) that a collection of ten billion grains of sand must not be a heap.

■ **soul (Gk. yuch [psychê]; Lat. anima)**

the active principle present in living things. Plato distinguished three distinct components of the human soul and Aristotle supposed that plants and animals, no less than human beings, have souls of some sort. Under the influence of Christianity, mediaeval philosophers focussed on the intellectual component of the human soul and Descartes identified it as an immaterial substance.

■ sound/unsound

distinction among deductive arguments. A sound argument both has true premises and employs a valid inference, its conclusion must therefore be true. An unsound argument either has one or more false premises or relies upon an invalid inference, its conclusion may be either true or false.

■ Souvré, Madeleine de, Marquise de Sablé (1599-1678)

French intellectual leader. Madame de Sablé hosted an influential salon at Port-Royal and wrote Maximes et Pensees Diverses (Moral Maxims and Reflections) (1691) summarising her view of human nature.

■ speech acts

the complex group of things we typically perform when speaking. J. L. Austin famously distinguished the simple locutionary act of saying something meaningful, the force of the illocutionary act of employing this language for some purpose and the further perlocutionary act of having an actual effect on those who hear the utterance. Thus, for example, in saying (locution) to a friend, 'That's an ugly necktie', I may also insult him (illocution) and persuade him to dress differently (perlocution).

■ Spencer, Herbert (1820-1903)

English philosopher whose Education (1861) promoted a scientific approach to the creative development of intellect. In the systematic philosophical work that began with First Principles (1862), Spencer tried to generalise from Darwinian evolution a comprehensive account of progress in human knowledge, morality and society. The political views expressed in Man versus the State (1884) include a nearly absolute defence of individual liberty and a strict opposition to governmental interference.

■ **Spinoza, Baruch (1632-1677)**

Portuguese-Dutch Jewish philosopher who developed a monistic account of the universe as a single infinite substance (God or Nature), whose essential features flow with logical necessity and include, as modes, every finite being.

■ **square of opposition**

in traditional categorical logic, a diagram representing the logical relationships that hold among propositions of different forms with the same terms:

'All S are P.' (A)- - - - - - -(E)
'No S are P.'
| * * |
* *
| * * |
*
| * * |
* *
| * * |
'Some S are P.' (I)———(O)
'Some S are not P.'

In this square, the contradictories are across from each other diagonally, the contraries are across the top and the subcontraries across the bottom, and subalternation holds on each side.

■ **Staël-Holstein, Anne Louise Germaine Necker, Baronne de (1766-1817)**

French novelist, essayist and philosopher. Although her controversial political views were often condemned, Madame de Staël's De l'influence des passions sur le boneur des individuals et des nations (A Treatise on the Influence of the Passions on the Happiness of Individuals and of Nations) (1796) was the chief source of her generation's information about the philosophies of Rousseau and Kant, while her De l'Allemagne (On Germany) emphasised the work of Fichte, Schelling and the Romantics.

standard form

a consistent way of organising deductive arguments. The standard form for a categorical syllogism is: Major Premise, Minor Premise, Conclusion.

Stanton, Elizabeth Cady (1815-1902)

American journalist and political activist, author of Degradation of Disenfranchisement (1892) and The Woman's Bible (1898), where she postulated an androgynous deity and defended the historical reality of matriarchy. Stanton founded the National Woman's Suffrage Association and devoted her career to the abolition of slavery and to secure the rights of women to vote. Her speech 'Dare to Question' argues for a strict separation between church and state.

statement

the content of a declarative sentence employed in its typical use. A proposition.

statement constant

a symbol (usually uppercase letters such as A, B, C, etc.) used to represent a specific simple statement in the propositional calculus.

statement form

in the propositional calculus, a string of symbols including only statement variables and connectives (along with parenthetical punctuation) such that the substitution of a statement for each of its variables would result in a well-formed compound statement.

statement variable

a symbol (usually lowercase letters such as p, q, r, s, etc.) used to represent any statement whatsoever in the propositional calculus.

Stevenson, Charles Leslie (1908-1979)

American philosopher. Stevenson's 'The Emotive Meaning of Ethical Terms' (1937), 'Persuasive Definitions' (1938) and Ethics and Language (1944) developed emotivism as a meta-ethical theory, in which moral judgements invariably express and encourage human feelings of characteristic sorts. His papers are collected in Facts and Values (1963).

■ Stewart, Dugald (1753-1828)

Scottish philosopher whose Elements of the Philosophy of the Human Mind (1792) helped to perpetuate Reid's philosophy of common sense realism. Stewart was an influential teacher whose students included Benjamin Constant, James Mill and Walter Scott.

■ stipulative definition

the arbitrary assignment of meaning to a term not previously in use. Although it may be relatively inconvenient or useless, such a definition can never be mistaken or incorrect.

■ stoicism

school of philosophy organised at Athens in the third century B.C.E. by Zeno of Citium and Chrysippus. The stoics provided a unified account of the world that comprised formal logic, materialistic physics and naturalistic ethics. Later Roman stoics, including Seneca, Epictetus and Marcus Aurelius, emphasised more exclusively the development of recommendations for living in harmony with a natural world, over which one has no direct control.

■ Strawson, Peter F. (1919-)

British philosopher who applies the methods of analytic philosophy to traditional philosophical problems. Strawson criticised Russell's theory of descriptions in 'On Referring' (1950) and developed the notion of descriptive (as opposed to revisionary) metaphysics in reference to problem of reidentification of particulars in Individuals: An Essay in Descriptive Metaphysics (1959). His The Bounds of Sense (1966) is an extended commentary on the critical philosophy of Kant.

■ structuralism

method of interpreting social phenomena in the context of a system of signs whose significance lies solely in the interrelationships among them. Initiated in the linguistics of

Saussure and Chomsky, structuralism was applied to other disciplines by Lévi-Strauss, Piaget, Althusser, Lacan, Barthes, Foucault and Eco. Most structuralists share a conviction that individual human beings function solely as elements of the (often hidden) social networks to which they belong.

Suárez, Francisco (1548-1617)

Spanish philosopher and theologian whose rejection of Aristotelean authority in the Disputationes Metaphysicae (Metaphysical Disputations) (1597) became a significant component of much Renaissance thinking. In De legibus ac Deo legislatore (On Law) (1612), Suárez qualified the natural law theory of Aquinas, defending instead a voluntaristic notion of the effect of legislative edicts.

■ subalternation

in the traditional square of opposition, the relationship between a universal proposition and its corresponding particular proposition. Thus, an I is the subaltern of its A proposition and an O is the subaltern of its E proposition. Thus, for example:

Some larks are birds is subaltern to All larks are birds, and. Some robins are not fish is subaltern to No robins are fish.

Subalternation is a reliable pattern of inference, only on the assumption of existential import for universal propositions.

■ subcontraries

a pair of categorical propositions which (provided that we

assume existential import) cannot both be false, although both could be true. In the traditional square of opposition, an I proposition and its corresponding O are subcontraries. Thus, for example: 'Some business leaders are women and Some business leaders are not women' are subcontraries.

■ **subjective**

that which depends upon the personal or individual, especially where, in contrast with the objective, it is supposed to be an arbitrary expression of private taste.

■ **sublime**

the aesthetic feeling aroused by experiences too overwhelming in scale to be appreciated as beautiful by the senses. The awe produced by standing on the brink of the Grand Canyon or the terror, induced by witnessing a hurricane, are properly said to be sublime.

■ **sub specie aeternitatis**

Latin for 'under the aspect of eternity'. Hence, from Spinoza onwards, an honorific expression describing what is universally and eternally true, without any reference to or dependence upon the merely temporal portions of reality.

■ **substance (Gk. ousia [ousia], Lat. substantia)**

what a thing is made of, hence, the underlying being that supports, exists independently of and persists through time despite changes in its accidental features. Aristotle identified substance, both primary and secondary, as the most fundamental of the ten categories of being. According to Spinoza, there can be no more than one truly independent being in the universe.

■ **substitution-instance**

a statement or argument that results from a consistent substitution of constants for variables in a statement form or argument form of the propositional calculus or quantification theory.

■ **sufficient condition**

what logically or causally secures the occurrence of something else. Thus, Leibniz supposed that there must always be a sufficient reason for the way things are.

sui generis

Latin for 'of its own kind', hence, whatever is absolutely unique or distinctive about something.

summum bonum

Latin phrase meaning 'highest good'. Hence, that which is intrinsically valuable, the ultimate goal or end of human life generally.

supererogatory

above and beyond the call of duty. Although agents are not obliged by the dictates of ordinary morality to perform supererogatory acts, extraordinary feats of heroism or extreme deeds of self-sacrifice, for example, they may be commended for doing so. Normative theories that demand the performance of the best possible action in every circumstance render supererogation impossible by identifying the permissible with the obligatory.

supervenient

belonging to or characteristic of something only in virtue of its having other features. Although a supervenient property cannot be defined in terms of, or reduced to, the properties on which it supervenes, nothing possesses (or can possess) those properties without also having it. In this sense, Hare supposed that moral properties are supervenient with respect to straightforward descriptions of human conduct, and Davidson proposes that mental events supervene on physical events.

syllogism

an important variety of deductive argument in which a conclusion follows from two or more premises, especially the categorical syllogism.

symbolic logic

the systematic representation of logic.

symbols, logical

connectives of the propositional calculus and the quantifiers of quantification theory employ the following logical symbols:

~ negation (x) universal quantifier.

conjunction ($x) existential quantifier.
Ú disjunction.
É material implication.
º material equivalence.

syncategorematic

not included among the categories of Aristotle and therefore incapable of serving as a categorical term. Hence, any linguistic expression that does not refer to anything else. Thus, 'if', 'while', and 'and', are all syncategorematic terms.

synderesis

immediate, intuitive apprehension of the fundamental principles of morality. For such mediaeval ethicists as Peter Lombard and Aquinas, synderesis, unlike mere conscience, is both infallible and general.

synonymous

having exactly the same meaning in more than one use. See **homonymous / synonymous / paronymous**. Although many since Aristotle have supposed this to be essential for effective communication, Quine has shown that the indeterminacy of translation renders genuine synonymy difficult to secure.

syntactics

study of the grammatical relationships among signs, independently of their interpretation or meaning, which is the subject of semantics.

synthesis

the combination or reconciliation of opposed notions.

synthetic

affirming a genuine connection between otherwise independent notions.

Tarski, Alfred (1902-1983)

Polish-American logician who defended a correspondence theory of truth, in The Concept of Truth in Formalized Languages (1933) and The Semantic Conception of Truth and the Foundations of Semantics (1944). According to Tarski, we must distinguish between a formal language and its interpretation as applicable within a specific domain, in order to define the truth of propositions within the formal language in terms of their satisfaction by the external conditions that obtain. Tarski's logical papers were collected in A Decision Method for Elementary Algebra and Geometry (1948) and Logic, Semantics, Metamathematics (1956).

■ tautology

1. logical truth, a statement which is necessarily true because, by virtue of its logical form, it cannot be used to make a false assertion. Example: 'If neither John nor Betty is here, then John is not here.'

2. a rule of replacement of the forms:

p ° (p Ú p).

p ° (p · p).

Example: 'Paul is tall.' is equivalent to 'Paul is tall and Paul is tall.' Although its ordinary-language use invariably seems pointless and redundant, this pattern of reasoning is a useful principle in the rigorous development of the propositional calculus.

■ Taylor, Harriet Hardy (1807-1858)

English philosopher. In The Enfranchisement of Women (1851), Taylor argued that the confinement of women to domestic pursuits was harmful to all human beings. She wrote eloquently on behalf of voting rights for women, equal opportunities in education and employment, and the abolition of restrictive laws governing marriage and divorce. Through her long and intimate association with John Stuart Mill, Taylor significantly contributed to the application of utilitarian principles to social and political issues.

■ tecnh (technê)

Greek term for the art, craft or skill, involved in deliberately producing something (poihsiV [poiêsis]), by contrast with those things that merely derive from nature (fusiV [physis]) or chance (tuch [tychê]). Both Plato and Aristotle distinguished its productive and practical components from more theoretical concerns.

■ teleological argument

an attempt to prove the existence of God, based upon an observation of the regularity or beauty of the universe. As employed by Cicero, Aquinas and Paley, the argument maintains that many aspects of the natural world exhibit an orderly and purposive character that would be most naturally explained by reference to the intentional design of an intelligent creator. Hume pointed out that since we have no experience of universe-formation generally, supposed inferences to its cause are unwarranted. Moreover, Darwin's theory of natural selection offered an alternative, non-teleological account of biological adaptations. In addition, anyone who accepts this line of argument but acknowledges the presence of imperfection in the natural order is faced with the problem of evil. Nevertheless, reasoning of this sort remains a popular pastime among convinced theists.

■ teloV (télos)

Greek term for the end, completion, purpose or goal of any thing or activity. According to Aristotle, this is the final cause which accounts for the existence and nature of a thing. Following Wolff, modern philosophers (often pejoratively) designate as teleological any explanation, theory or argument that emphasises purpose.

■ Teresa of Ávila (Teresa Sánchez de Cepeda y Ahumada) (1515-1582)

Spanish mystic. Teresa's The Way of Perfection (1566) and The Interior Castle, sharply distinguished intellectual from volitional portions of human nature and recommended the total surrender of the soul to god through both prayerful meditation and ecstatic union with the divine.

■ terminus a quo / terminus ad quem

Latin phrases for 'limit from which' and 'limit to which'. Hence, the temporal starting-point and ending-point for the occurrence of any event, the moments of its beginning and its completion.

■ Thales (c. 585 BCE)

presocratic philosopher who first proposed rational explanation of the natural world. In fragmentary reports from other philosophers, Thales is supposed to have held that 'All is water.' His Milesian followers commonly disagreed with this simple identification of the arch (archê).

■ theism

belief in the existence of god as a perfect being deserving of worship.

■ theodicy

an attempt to explain or defend the perfect benevolence of God despite the apparent presence of evil in the world. In this vein, for example, Leibniz devoted great effort to demonstrating that this is the best of all possible worlds.

■ theoretical definition

a proposal for understanding the meaning of a term in relation to a set of scientifically useful hypothesis.

■ thesis / antithesis / synthesis

in the philosophy of Hegel, the inevitable transition of thought, by contradiction and reconciliation, from an initial conviction to its opposite and then to a new, higher conception that involves but transcends both of them. Thus, for example:

Being / Non-being / Becoming,

subjective / objective / absolute, or.

symbolic / classical / romantic.

Since he identified reality with thought, Hegel believed that the same triadic movement is to be found in nature, cultural progress and history.

■ thing-in-itself (Ger. Ding an sich)

an object as it is (or would be) independently of our awareness of it, the noumenon. As Kant showed, we cannot know things-in-themselves but can only postulate their nature from what we know about observable phenomena.

■ **Thomas Aquinas**

Italian Dominican philosopher and theologian.

■ **Thomson, Judith Jarvis (1929-)**

American moral philosopher; author of Acts and Other Events (1977), The Realm of Rights (1990) and Moral Realtivism and Moral Objectivity (1996). In Rights, Restitution, and Risk: Essays in Moral Theory (1986), Thomson develops an ethical stance grounded upon the defeasible presumption of individual rights. Thomson's A Defence of Abortion (1971) famously establishes that termination of pregnancy, under certain circumstances, is morally permissible even if the foetus is granted status as a person entitled to rights. Abortion (1995) offers her more recent reflections on the same subject.

■ **Thoreau, Henry David (1817-1862)**

American writer. Thoreau's essay 'On Civil Disobedience' (1849) is a classic statement of the principles, later employed by Gandhi and King, of passive resistance against governmental authority, on the basis of individual conscience.

■ **Tillich, Paul (1886-1965)**

German-American theologian. Tillich's Systematic Theology (1951-1964) defines religion as the most ultimate of all human concerns, identifies God with the ground of all being, and treats religious language and ritual as symbolic. In The Courage to Be (1952), Tillich employed central concepts from existentialism, to recommend a life of personal authenticity in the face of cultural and political obstacles.

■ time (Ger. Zeit)

temporal duration. Philosophers have traditionally addressed such questions as: whether time is an independent feature of reality or merely an aspect of our experience, whether or not it makes sense to think of time as having had a beginning, why time is directional and the past and future are asymmetrical, whether time flows continuously or is composed of discrete moments, whether there is absolute time in addition to relations of temporal succession and whether it is possible to travel through time.

The Eleatics developed general arguments to show that time and motion are impossible, and Augustine employed the analysis of time to explain human freedom in the face of divine power. Leibniz maintained that time is nothing more than temporal relations, Newton and Clarke defended its absolute character and Kant tried to mediate by regarding space and time as pure forms of sensible intuition. Later idealists commonly followed McTaggart in denying the reality of time.

■ timh (timê)

Greek term for honour, esteem or dignity. Thus, for Plato, a timocratic society or person is unduly governed by concern for public dignity or reputation.

■ time travel

the philosophy of time travel assumes that travel to the past is physically possible and proceeds to discuss the philosophical consequences of this assumption:

· *Changing The Past*: If it is possible to return to the past, then it follows that it is possible to change the past. If the past is changed, then something both did and did not happen and this is a contradiction.

There is Nowhere to Go: Time travel to the past assumes that times are, in some sense, still there. If not, there is simply no destination for the time traveller.

Causal Anomalies: Time travel opens up the apparent possibility for anomalous causal chains. Typical examples in the literature are being your own parent or sending back photographs of Van Gogh's paintings to Van Gogh, as a ten year old. These causal anomalies, though strange, do not appear to be contradictory.

Self Defeating Causal Chains: If time travel is possible, then this entails the possibility of a causal chain cancelling itself out, as when returning to your past and killing your infant self.

To the above objections to time travel there are many counter-arguments in the literature.

■ Timon of Philius (320-230 BCE)

Greek sceptic who expounded and defended the views of Pyrrhonism by offering satirical commentary on the works of Plato, Aristotle and other Greek philosophers.

■ token

a particular instance of a word or sign, as opposed to the abstract kind or type it exemplifies. Thus, for example, the preceding sentence is 18 words long (token), but contains only 16 words (type), since 'a' and 'or' are each used twice.

■ Toland, John (1670-1722)

English philosopher. Toland's Christianity not Mysterious (1696) offered a purely rational defence of God's existence and relation to the natural world, marking a transition between the philosophy of John Locke and the rise of Deism.

■ transcendental argument

reasoning from the fact that we do have experiences or engage in practices of a certain sort to the truth of those conditions without which these experiences or practices would not be possible. Kant employed transcendental arguments to establish our synthetic yet a priori knowledge of mathematics and natural science as features of the world as it appears to us. Strawson employs a similar pattern of reasoning to show that our identification of particulars presupposes the existence of material objects.

■ **transposition (trans.)**
a rule of replacement of the form:
(p É q) º (~ q É ~ p).
Example: 'If it produces pleasure, then it is right.' is equivalent to 'If it isn't right, then it doesn't produce pleasure.'
A simple truth-table shows the reliability of inferences of this sort.

■ **Trotsky, Leon (Lev Davidovich Bronstein) (1879-1940)**
Russian social and political philosopher who participated in the Bolshevik revolution but was later exiled by Stalin. Although he often expressed respect for the psychological theories of Freud, Trotsky's effort to establish philosophical foundations for the political theories of Marx in the later book In Defence of Marxism, emphasised a narrow reliance on dialectical materialism as a comprehensive view of social reality.

■ **truth (Gk. alhqeia [alêtheia], Lat. veritas, Ger. Wahrheit)**
the conformity of a proposition to the way things are. Precise analysis of the nature of truth is the subject of the correspondence, coherence, pragmatic, redundancy and semantic theories of truth.

■ **truth-functional**
a compound statement or connective is truth-functional if its truth or meaning is wholly determined by the possible combinations of truth-value of its component statements.

■ **truth-table**

a simple chart showing the possible combinations of truth-values for a statement form or an argument form in the propositional calculus.

■ **Truth, Sojourner (Isabella Baumfree van Wagener) (1797-1883)**

American advocate for human rights. After her emancipation from slavery, Sojourner Truth became famous as public speaker. One of her best-known orations is Ain't I a Woman? (1851), an eloquent plea for recognition of the dignity of working-class women. The Narrative of Sojourner Truth, a Bondswoman of Olden Time (dictated to Olive Gilbert in 1850) is a clear statement of her principled defence of women's rights, temperance and the abolition of slavery.

■ **tuch (tychê)**

Greek term for fortune, luck or chance, as opposed to the necessity (Gk. anagkh [anankê]) of logical or causal connections. In moral life, especially, this significantly diminishes the tendency of virtue to produce happiness with any regularity or certainty.

■ **tu quoque**

the informal fallacy of replying to criticism by arguing that one's opponent is guilty of something equally improper. Example: 'Republicans claim that Democrats make illegal use of campaign funds. But they do the same thing themselves, so there is no reason to enforce campaign finance laws.' This fallacy is usefully regarded as a special case of the circumstantial ad hominem argument.

■ **Turing, Alan Mathison (1912-1954)**

English mathematician. Extrapolating from the mathematical discoveries of Gödel, Turing proposed in Computing Machinery and Intelligence (1950), a specific description of just what an idealised machine could, in principle, compute. In addition to its practical importance for the development of digital computing equipment, Turing's theory provides support for a functionalist account of the mind, by proposing the practical test of whether or not we would attribute intelligence to a system whose performance is indistinguishable from that of a human agent.

■ type / token

a distinction, first drawn by Peirce, between signs considered as abstract things (types) or as particular instances (tokens). Thus, for example, the number of words (tokens) in this Dictionary, the 'word-count' of its content, may be quite large, but the number of different words (types) it uses, the working vocabulary of its author, is surely much smaller.

The distinction is also used by Davidson and other philosophers of mind to emphasise that a reasonable identity theory need only argue for the identity of mental and physical events as types, not necessarily as tokens.

■ types, theory of

the solution proposed by Russell for the self-referential paradox that arises from the notion of 'the class of all classes that are not members of themselves'. Russell envisioned an indefinite hierarchy of types to be symbolised: ordinary objects, the properties and relations of ordinary objects, the features of properties of objects, etc. Defining each item by reference only to those of a lower type avoids paradox, but may not resolve every instance of difficulty with self-reference.

■ Übermensch

German term for 'Overman' or 'Superman'. Hence, in the

philosophy of Nietzsche, an extraordinary individual who transcends the limits of traditional morality to live purely by the will to power.

■ Unamuno, Miguel de (1864-1936)

Spanish philosopher. In Del sentimento trágico de la vida en los hombres y en los pueblos (The Tragic Sense of Life) (1913), Unamuno described human existence as torn between the irrational hope for immortality and the rational expectation of death. Since faith can never outweigh reason, Unamuno supposed the best we can achieve is a life of authentic struggle with the human predicament.

■ unconscious

mental activity of which the person engaging in it is not aware. Hence, a presumed source of unknown internal influences, over the conduct of human agent. Psychoanalysts like Freud, Jung and Lacan supposed it possible to discover the content and significance of such influences with suitable methods of psychoanalytic investigation.

■ underdetermination

the characteristic of rival hypothesis, each of which is consistent with the available evidence. The possibility that every scientific theory must always remain undetermined, raises significant doubt about the success of abductive reasoning.

■ understanding (Gk. dianoia [diánoia], Lat. ingenium, Ger. Verstehen)

the human capacity for comprehending the nature of reality. In Plato's theory of knowledge, we comprehend the truths of mathematics through understanding. For modern philosophers following Descartes or Locke, the understanding is the intellectual faculty considered more broadly or generally.

■ undistributed middle

the formal fallacy committed in a categorical syllogism that is invalid because its middle term is not distributed in either premise. Example: All dogs are mammals. Some mammals are whales. Therefore, some dogs are whales.

■ uniformity of nature

presumption that the future will be like the past, assumption that the world exhibits enough regularity to warrant inductive reasoning. Hume pointed out that such uniformity is presupposed by all of our belief in matters of fact, Mill identified several practical methods for recognising its instances, but Goodman raised a significant paradox of induction.

■ Universal Generalisation (U.G.)

inference from the features of a representative individual to a general truth about everything of the same sort, hence, a quantification rule of the form:

Øy.

(x)(Øx).

Example: 'Any arbitrarily chosen spaniel must also be a dog. Therefore, all spaniels are dogs.'

With appropriate qualifications, this pattern of reasoning provides an important basis for proofs in quantification theory.

■ Universal Instantiation (U.I.)

inference from a general truth about everything to its application to an individual, hence, a quantification rule of the form:

(x)(Øx).

Øu.

Example: 'All dogs are mammals. Therefore, if Chloë is a dog, then Chloë is a mammal.' This pattern of reasoning is one of the basic principles used by proofs in quantification theory.

■ universal proposition

a statement whose propositional quantity is determined by its assertion that all members of one class of things are either included or excluded from membership in some other class.

Examples: 'All spaniels are dogs.' and 'No wristwatches are nuclear weapons.' are both universal.

Although it is often difficult in practice to establish the truth of universal propositions, those that are accepted have extensive deductive consequences.

■ universals, problem of

universals are features (e.g., redness or tallness) shared by many individuals, each of which is said to instantiate or exemplify the universal. Although it began with dispute over the status of Platonic Forms, the problem of universals became a central concern during the Middle Ages. The metaphysical issue is whether or not these features exist independently of the particular things that have them: realists hold that they do, nominalists hold that they do not, conceptualists hold that they do so only mentally.

■ universalisability

the applicability of a moral rule to all similarly situated individuals. According to both Kant and Hare, universalisability is a distinguishing feature of moral judgements and a substantive guide to moral obligation: moral imperatives must be regarded as equally binding on everyone. The force of this principle, however, depends upon the generality of the judgements and the particularity of the situations to which they are applied.

■ univocal / equivocal

distinction among statements, expressions and terms: those are univocal which have only one meaning, ambiguous terms are equivocal, having more than one meaning.

■ Ursache

German term for cause.

■ Urteil

German term for judgement.

■ use/mention

distinction between two ways of employing a word or phrase: in order to refer to something else (use) or in order to draw attention to its own features (mention). Sarah does well in chemistry. uses the name 'Sarah,' but 'Sarah' is an anagram for 'a rash' merely mentions it. Thus, the first proposition expresses a truth about Sarah, while the second merely points out an odd feature of her name.

■ utilitarianism

normative theory that human conduct is right or wrong because of its tendency to produce favourable or unfavourable consequences for the people who are affected by it. The hedonistic utilitarianism of Bentham, Mill and Sidgwick maintains that all moral judgements can be derived from the greatest happiness principle. The ideal utilitarianism espoused by G. E. Moore, on the other hand, regarded aesthetic enjoyment and friendship as the highest ethical values. Contemporary utilitarians differ about whether the theory should be applied primarily to acts or rules.

■ vagueness

the characteristic of words or phrases whose meaning is not determined with precision. Use of one or more vague terms typically renders it impossible to establish the truth or falsity of the sentences in which they appear. Example: 'The temperature is warm today' is difficult to evaluate because there is no clear borderline between 'warm' and 'not warm'. Note the difference between vagueness and ambiguity.

■ Vaihinger, Hans (1852-1933)

German philosopher. In Die Philosophie des Als-Ob (The Philosophy of As-If) (1911), Vaihinger extrapolated from Kant's epistemology (as understood by Schopenhauer) the notion that all of our concepts, including those involved in both science and morality, are nothing more than useful fictions. This outlook was a significant influence on the psychological theories of Alfred Adler. Vaihinger described the origins of his theory in Wie die

Philosophie des Als Ob entstand (1924).

■ **valid / invalid**

the most crucial distinction among deductive arguments and the inferences upon which they rely. In a valid argument, if the premises are true, then the conclusion must also be true. Alternatively, it is impossible for the premises of a valid argument to be true while its conclusion is false. All other arguments are invalid, that is, it is possible for their conclusions to be false even when their premises are true. Thus, even the most reliable instances of inductive reasoning fall short of deductive validity.

■ **Valla, Lorenzo (1407-1457)**

a leader of the Italian Renaissance. Valla's humanistic philosophy criticised the sterility of scholastic logical distinctions and tried to synthesise Christian principles with Stoic and Epicurean thought. In De libero arbitratio (Of Free Choice), Valla noted the incompatibility of divine omnipotence with human freedom.

■ **value (Ger. Wert)**

worth in some respect, which may be either intrinsic or extrinsic to the things that have it. The most general philosophical issue in the study of value (axiology) is whether values arise from objective or subjective features of experience. Noncognitivists defend a strict distinction between fact and value, and many contemporary thinkers challenge the presumption that human knowledge can ever be genuinely free of value-judgements.

■ **variable**

in a system of formal logic, any symbol that, unlike a constant, designates generally. Thus, the propositional calculus employs statement variables, while quantification theory makes use of individual variables.

■ **Veblen, Thorsten (1857-1929)**

American social philosopher whose work contributed to the sociology of knowledge, by emphasising the influence of material conditions on the development of human thought. Veblen's critical analysis of American capitalism is evident in The Theory of the Leisure Class (1899) and The Higher Learning in America (1918) comments on the devastating effect of treating higher education as a business.

■ Venn, John (1834-1923)
British logician. In Symbolic Logic (1881), Venn applied the insights of Boole, Euler and others, in developing a diagrammatic method for testing the validity of categorical syllogisms. He also contributed to the development of modern theories of probability in The Logic of Chance (1867) and The Principles of Empirical or Inductive Logic (1889).

■ Venn diagrams
John Venn's modern pictorial method of representing and evaluating the validity of categorical syllogisms. The classes designated by the terms of a syllogism are represented by overlapping circles, with shading and ×s, indicating, respectively, the impossibility and existence of their common members.

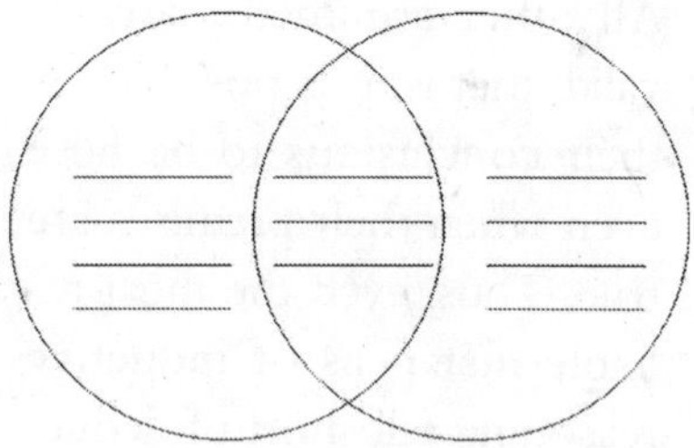

■ verbal dispute
the appearance of disagreement between parties who have not resolved the ambiguity of one or more key terms. Agreement on the definition of these terms eliminates a verbal dispute completely.

■ verecundiam, argumentum ad
the fallacy of making an illicit appeal to authority.

■ **verifiability principle**

the claim that the meaning of a proposition is just the set of observations or experiences which would determine its truth, so that an empirical proposition is meaningful only if it either actually has been verified or could at least in principle be verified. (Analytic statements are non-empirical, their truth or falsity requires no verification.) Verificationism was an important element in the philosophical programme of logical positivism.

■ **veritas**

Latin word for truth.

■ **Vernunft**

German term for reason. Kant distinguished reine Vernunft ('pure reason') or abstract thought from praktische Vernunft ('practical reason') or volition.

■ **Verstehen**

German term for understanding.

■ **Vico, Giambattista (1668-1744)**

Italian philosopher. In Principi di una scienza nuova d'intorno alla comune natura delle nazioni (Principles of a New Science of the Common Nature of Nations) (1725), Vico argued that study of the cycles exhibited in human history rests on a foundation and methodology (distinct from that pursued by the natural sciences), under which the genius of each age must be understood in its own terms alone. This position was a significant influence on the work of Hegel, Marx and Croce.

■ **Vienna Circle**

a group of philosophers, mathematicians and scientists in Austria, during the 1920s and early 1930s, who founded logical positivism with their joint publication of Wissenschaftliche Weltauffassung—der Wiener

Kreis (A Scientific World-view—The Vienna Circle) in 1929. Members of the Circle included Carnap, Feigl, Gödel, Hahn, Neurath, Schlick and Waismann. Schlick died in 1936 and the others all left for England or the United States by 1938.

■ **virtue (Gk. areth [aretê], Lat. virtus)**

excellence, skill or art. In classical thought, virtues are admirable human characteristics or dispositions that distinguish good people from bad. Socrates sought a singular virtue for human life, while Plato identified four central virtues present in the ideal state or person. Aristotle held that every moral virtue is the mean between vicious extremes. Modern deontologists and utilitarians tend to suppose that individual virtues are morally worthwhile only when they encourage the performance of duty or contribute to the general welfare.

■ **virtue ethics**

normative theory that all moral value is derived from the character of moral agents. Aristotle and many medieval Christians assumed that the acquisition of virtue is the proper goal of human conduct, though they differed significantly in their valuation of particular virtues. Rejecting the impersonality of moral judgements in the ethical theories of Kant and Mill, contemporary virtue ethicists emphasise the achievement of a meaningful life.

■ **volition**

exercise of the faculty of willing. The supposition that an act of volition is a necessary precondition, for any voluntary action notoriously leads to an infinite regress in explaining the voluntary nature of the volition itself.

■ **volonté générale**

Rousseau's French term for the general will that properly guides the decisions of a civil society, rather than the sum of their individual self-interests, the volonté de tous.

■ **Voltaire François Marie Arouet (1694-1778)**

French philosopher. Like the other Encyclopaedists, Voltaire greatly admired the philosophy of John Locke and he defended his own version of sensationalism in the Dictionnaire Philosophique (Philosophical Dictionary) (1764) and Lettres Philosophiques (Letters Concerning the English Nation) (1734). As a freethinker and deist, Voltaire opposed institutional religion generally. In Poème sur la Désastre de Lisbonne (On the Lisbon Disaster) (1756) and Candide, ou l'optimisme (Candide) (1759), Voltaire's acknowledgement of the presence of evil grounded a bitter rejection of Leibniz's conviction that God has created the best of all possible worlds.

■ **voluntarism**

belief that the nature of reality, the principles of morality or the structure of society derives from the determinations of human or (especially) divine will.

■ **voluntary / involuntary**

in moral philosophy since Aristotle, the distinction between actions that are freely performed in accordance with determination of the will of a moral agent and those which are produced by force or ignorance.

■ **Von Neumann, John (1903-1957)**

Hungarian-American mathematician whose work included study of mathematical logic, set theory and game theory. The complex calculations required for work on weapons systems led to the invention of modern computing machinery and von Neumann was the first to devise a functional set of program instructions for an electronic computer. Any device that sequentially reads and performs a stored program, providing for input and output, through a central processing unit, is commonly called a 'von Neumann machine'.

■ voting paradox

a systematic difficulty with the attempt to make consistent social choices by majority rule. Suppose that among three options, equal portions of the population rank them 1-2-3, 2-3-1 and 3-1-2. Then, even though the relative preferences seem rational and evenly divided, in head-to-head competitions, two-thirds of the voters favour 1 over 2 and two-thirds 2 over 3, yet two-thirds favour 3 over 1. Although several Enlightenment thinkers had pointed out similar difficulties in the foundations of social contract theory, twentieth-century economist Kenneth Arrow demonstrated formally that the collective preferences of groups cannot always be determined from the individual preferences of their members.

■ Wahrheit

German term for truth.

■ Waismann, Friedrich (1896-1959)

Austrian philosopher. One of the original members of the Vienna Circle gathering of logical positivists, Waismann defended a conventionalist logic in Einführung in das mathematische Denken (An Introduction to Mathematical Thinking) (1936). Sprachspiele und Vagheit der Sprache and his later lectures, published posthumously as The Principles of Linguistic Philosophy (1965), contributed to the development of analytic philosophy by encouraging serious analysis of ordinary language. Waismann held that even precisely defined terms have an 'open texture', since novel circumstances might always render their application uncertain.

■ Watson, John Broadus (1878-1958)

American psychologist whose Psychology from the Standpoint of a Behaviourist (1913) and Behaviour: an Introduction to Comparative Psychology (1914) founded modern behaviourism by requiring that the science of psychology study only public, external stimuli and responses, rather than appeal to the introspection of putatively private, internal experiences.

■ weakness of will (Gk. akrasia [akrásia])
inability to carry out an action in accordance with reason or virtue. Socrates held that agents never knowingly do wrong, but Aristotle maintained that the influence of the passions often results in incontinence.

■ Weber, Max (1864-1920)
German social theorist who developed many of the principles of the modern discipline of sociology. He is the author of Sociology as Science (1897) and Methodology of the Social Sciences (1907). Weber argued for a strict separation between scientific objectivity and all judgements of value in Die 'Objectivität' sozialwissenschaftlicher und sozialpolitischer Erkentniss (The 'Objectivity' of Knowledge in Social Science and Social Policy) (1904). Ultimately, Weber supposed, ethical and political commitments are properly embraced without any effort to supply their rational foundations. In Die protestantische Ethik und der Geist des Kapitalismus (The Protestant Ethic and the Spirit of Capitalism) (1905), Weber warned against the loss of individual freedom to the

efficient but over-rationalised bureaucracy that arises in service of economic investment.

■ Weil, Simone (1909-1943)

French philosopher and mystic, author of Waiting for God, Gravity and Grace and Leçons de Philosophie). (Lectures on Philosophy. Following her conversion to Christianity in 1938, Weil argued in Intimations of Christianity Among the Ancient Greeks, that its central theological themes could be discerned by a careful reader in the philosophical works of Plato and other Greek sages. In Oppression et liberté (Oppression and Liberty) (1955), Weil argued that individuals can overcome the alienation characteristic of modern society only through their engagement in meaningful work.

■ well-formed formula

any expression that satisfies the recursive formation rules for the introduction of compound statements in a formal system for symbolic logic.

■ Weltanschauung

German term for 'World-view', a general outlook on human life and its place in the greater order of the universe.

■ Wert

German term for value. Max Weber held that all social science is properly Wertfrei ('value-free').

■ West, Cornel (1953-)

American theologian and social philosopher, whose The American Evasion of Philosophy: A Genealogy of Pragmatism (1989) traces the origins of American thought in the work of Emerson and Thoreau. In The Ethical Dimensions of Marxist Thought (1991) and Race Matters (1993), West addresses the significance of racial concerns in contemporary American culture.

■ Whewell, William (1794-1866)

British philosopher of science. In the Philosophy of the Inductive Sciences, Founded upon Their History (1840) and The Plurality of Worlds (1858), Whewell defended a hypothetico-deductive model of Baconian natural science, emphasising the role of intellectual creativity in theory-formation and defending a strict scientific realism in opposition to the strictly empiricist views of Mill. Thus, he held that Newton mechanics for celestial and terrestrial motion provides necessary truths about the structure of the universe. Whewell considered the implications of this view for ethics in The Elements of Morality (1856).

■ **Whitehead, Alfred North (1861-1947)**

English mathematician and philosopher who collaborated with Russell on Principia Mathematica (1910-13). After a long career in mathematics at Cambridge and London, Whitehead accepted a position in philosophy at Harvard in 1924. In Process and Reality (1929), he developed an abstract methodology through which to propose a comprehensive metaphysical view, according to which events and processes, rather than independent substances, constitute reality. This view points toward the progressive development of conscious organic beings mutually involved in prehensive relations to each other.

■ **Wiener Kreis**

Group of Austrian analytical philosophers known (in English) as the Vienna Circle.

■ **will**

the faculty of deciding, choosing or acting.

■ **Wilson, Edward Osborne (1929-)**

American biologist, author of Sociobiology: The New Synthesis (1975) and On Human Nature (1978). Extrapolating from his zoological studies, Wilson promotes the discipline of 'sociobiology', offering explanations of human social behaviour in strictly biological terms. In Biophilia (1986) Wilson proposes that human appreciation of the natural world is an innate expression of a vital biological aspect of our evolutionary development.

■ Wilson, John Cook (1849-1915)

English logician and philosopher. Although he had studied with Green, Cook Wilson rejected idealism in favour of a realistic epistemology. His classroom teaching and posthumously collected papers, Statement and Inference were influential on a generation of Oxford philosophers.

■ Wirklichkeit

German term for reality.

■ Wirkung

German term for effect.

■ wisdom (Gk. sofia [sophía], Lat. sapientia)

good judgement with respect to abstract truth or theoretical matters (in contrast to prudence in concrete, practical affairs). For Plato, wisdom is the virtue appropriate to the rational soul and for Aristotle, it is the highest intellectual virtue.

■ Wisdom, John (1904-1993)

British philosopher whose Other Minds (1952) and Philosophy and Psychoanalysis (1953) applied the analytic methods of Moore and the later Wittgenstein, to significant issues in the philosophy of mind.

■ Wissen

German term for knowledge.

■ Wittgenstein, Ludwig (1889-1951)

Austrian philosopher whose brilliant, aphoristic and controversial writings (in two distinct stages) provided the impetus for both logical positivism and linguistic analysis.

Wolff, Christian (1679-1754)

German philosopher who wrote in both Latin and German, developing an extensive philosophical nomenclature for his native tongue and introducing a style that insisted upon thorough treatment of every issue. Wolff developed a philosophical system similar to that of Leibniz in his Philosophia Prima sive Ontologia (First Philosophy, or Ontology) (1721). Although his rationalistic metaphysical doctrines were condemned for their fatalistic implications in ethics, they remained influential until subjected to Kant's critique.

Wollstonecraft, Mary (1759-1797)

English political writer. In A Vindication of the Rights of Woman (1792), Wollstonecraft argued that the natural development of human capacities has been significantly curtailed because of the domination of women by men.

Xenocrates (396-314 BCE)

Greek philosopher who defended the philosophy of Plato against the criticism of Aristotle. As the head of the Academy in the fourth century, Xenocrates held forth the quasi-Pythagorean view that the Platonic Forms, including even the individual human soul, are all numbers.

Xenophanes of Colophon (570-475 BCE)

pre-socratic philosopher. He criticised the militarism and anthropomorphism of traditional Greek morality and religion, arguing that fundamental truth about the world is difficult to achieve. His opposition to conventional notions earned him the respect of later, more completely sceptical thinkers. Parmenides and Zeno studied with Xenophanes in Sicily, before establishing their own school at Elea.

Xenophon (430-350 B.C.E.)

Greek historian. Xenophon's dialogues, especially the Apologhma (Apology) and Memorabilia, offer an account of the philosophical career of Socrates through more practical, worldly eyes than do the dialogues of Plato.

■ **Zeit**

German term for time. Thus die Zeitgeist or 'Spirit of the Age' is the set of conceptions characteristic of the thinkers of a particular era.

■ **Zeno of Citium (334-262 BCE)**

Greek philosopher. An early exponent of stoic philosophy, he devised its characteristic separation of logic, natural science and ethics. According to Zeno, only acceptance of objective reality permits human beings to overcome their subjective passions.

■ **Zeno of Elea (c. 450 BCE)**

follower of Parmenides whose work is known to us only through fragmentary reports from other philosophers. Zeno was the presocratic philosopher who devised clever paradoxes to show that motion of any kind is impossible and that reality must be unitary and unchanging.

■ **Zermelo, Ernst Friedrich Ferdinand (1871-1953)**

German mathematician who developed the first systematic axiomatisation of set theory. This achievement drew attention to the importance of the axiom of choice.

■ **zombie**

in contemporary discussions of the philosophy of mind, a hypothetical being whose appearance, behaviour and speech is indistinguishable from that of a normal human being, despite its total lack of conscious experience in any form.

33. Geology 125/-
34. Genetic Engineering 125/-
35. Health & Nutrition 125/-
36. History 125/-
37. Import and Export 125/-
38. Information System Management 125/-
39. Internet 125/-
40. IT 125/-
41. Inorganic Chemistry 125/-
42. Law 125/-
43. Library & Information Science 125/-
44. Literature 125/-
45. Management 125/-
46. Mathematics 125/-
47. Marketing & Sales 125/-
48. Mass Communication 125/-
49. Mechanical Engg. 125/-
50. Medical 125/-
51. Music 125/-
52. Organic Chemistry 125/-
53. Philosophy 125/-
54. Physical Education 125/-
55. Physics 125/-
56. Psychology 125/-
57. Science 125/-
58. Sex 125/-
59 Sociology 125/-
60. Sports 125/-
61. Textile 125/-
62. Zoology 125/-

Lotus PRESS

Unit No. 220, Second Floor, 4735/22,
Prakash Deep Building, Ansari Road, Darya Ganj,
New Delhi - 110002, Ph.: 32903912, 23280047, 09811594448
E-mail: lotuspress1984@gmall.com, www.lotuspress.co.in

Other Books on

LOTUS ILLUSTRATED DICTIONARIES

1. Dictionary of New Words (New)	125/-
2. Dictionary of Veterinary Sciences (New)	125/-
3. Dictionary of Synonyms and Antonyms (New)	150/-
4. Dictionary of Idioms and Phrases (New)	150/-
5. First English Dictionary	125/-
6. Astronomy	125/-
7. Agriculture	125/-
8. Anthropology	125/-
9. Archaeology	125/-
10. Architecture	125/-
11. Art	125/-
12. Banking Finance & Accounting	125/-
13. Bio-Chemistry	125/-
14. Business Administration	125/-
15. Bio-Technology	125/-
16. Biology	125/-
17. Botany	125/-
18. Culture	125/-
19. Chemical Engg.	125/-
20. Chemistry	125/-
21. Civil Engineering	125/-
22. Computer Science	125/-
23. Commerce	125/-
24. Cooking & Food	125/-
25. Ecology	125/-
26. Economics	125/-
27. Education	125/-
28. Electrical Engineering	125/-
29. Electronic & Telecommunication	125/-
30. Environmental Studies	125/-
31. Festival	125/-
32. Geography	125/-